UNDENIABLE

An Epic Journey Through Pain

Bryan C. Gallant

To my precious Penny . . .

You have defied the odds
in your life and in loving me.
Thank you for persisting
through all the challenges
we have faced through the years.
I look forward to growing old with you
and walking each step together ahead.
I love you and love being loved by you!

Table of Contents

Undeniable

Prologue

It always seems to rain when we visit. I expected the rain to begin any moment. As I drove, there seemed to be clouds hanging over us, holding all of our words. I stole a glance at Penny and saw that the turmoil rolling around in my mind was etched on her face as well. No audible thunder was heard outside yet, just the threatening of darkness. The minivan was quiet.

I parked on the side of the road along one of the minor arteries of the Waterford Township Cemetery, allowing us to have a short walk to that known place: a place I loved and hated. Each step closer stirred the confusion and pain in my heart.

As we passed the gravestones I experienced a war on my senses. The calm Michigan sunlight filtered through the vibrant trees while dancing off of the colorful flowers. There was the smell of manicured, freshly cut grass showing distinct care and invested energy. Even the various children's commemorative toys and bright, plastic spinners flirted with the breeze, making this place seem almost surreal. Each toy standing like a sentry holding onto memories, guarding them and seeming to deny what this place is: a dead place.

It was quiet, too quiet.

The gentle trill of a bird from above, an occasional passing vehicle, and the solemn sound of our steps just could not compete with the cry of my heart. The storm was about to burst. Penny and I walked side-by-side, reminded again of what it means to be alone because of death. We found the correct row, and pushed towards the back, finally arriving.

I held her as we looked down at the gravestone that marked the resting place of our precious children, Caleb and Abigail, both of them having died together, long before their time in 1994.

Emotions erupted as I was again face to granite face with this reminder of our pain and loss. Questions exploded like lightning and assaulted me again, each piercing my thoughts with one little word, "why?"

The thunder of raw emotions shook me from inside my very core.

Why?

Below us were the bodies of our children, like discarded actors in the play we call life; snuffed out in an early exit with no encore, no matter how hard and long we screamed for it!

Why did they die so young? Why them and not us? The questions clamored over each other in my mind. Waves of pain washed over me with each yearning thought.

The rain burst, streamed down our cheeks, and mingled with our tears.

Penny returned my hug with her own clinging embrace. There was nothing else we could do except hold onto each other.

Memories flooded back. Grief surged. Anger screamed. The quicksand of questions pulled at me again and again, the relentless vacuum threatening to pull me under. I held Penny tighter, hoping that together we might survive. Time seemed to stand still in the agony.

Crumbling under the unseen weight, we collapsed and grasped at the picture of our precious babies which was fixed to the granite in an acrylic enclosure. We wept.

The faded picture matched my now fading memories. I saw Caleb's childlike smile looking at his sister, Abigail. Gentle, yet intent, like the protective older brother he was, sitting behind her, encouraging her to hold her ever-present smile for the photographer of years gone by. Both of them were wearing their church clothes, the nicest we could afford on my limited income back then.

As I looked at the picture I tried to convince myself to remember their living faces wearing the bright colors and rouse a nice memory to match. But all I could see was that day they died in front of me—wearing those same, exact clothes! The colors repulsed me.

After some agonizing moments I whispered something nonsensical and tried to tidy up the place a bit. Penny joined me in moving the leaves, trying to clean around the acrylic picture as best she could with only one working hand since the fateful day of the accident, her own daily reminder of loss, change and death. We worked together trying to make this hallowed and painful place look a little nicer.

I stroked Penny's hair and wiped a tear from her eye. Here was my precious bride of more than twenty years. I didn't know her exact thoughts at that moment, but seeing her weeping hinted at the deep anguish that was tearing her apart; her loss of memory of that day, her battle to live and hold cherished memories. Here was the amazing woman I love, who nearly died that day as well.

As I looked at her, my mind ran forwards and backwards trying to take it all in. We were so young when the children died. We had started our marriage young and unaware, and yet, we went through so much together in the years that followed. In spite of the pain, we had fought to live. We had fought with each other and with the grief trying to rob us of life. We had learned to live and love again after being nearly decimated by the date etched in the rock before us.

Calling me back to this time and place, she looked at me and the words barely escaped her quivering lips, "Were we good parents?"

Another lightning bolt. Why is it that death causes such painful reflection and questions of ultimate worth?

She struggled again, pushing the words out, her voice breaking, "Did they know we loved them?"

The guilt of those who survive is not easy to carry.

"Yes," I wanted to scream! She had been a good mother, she had done her best and they knew they were loved.

But, I, on the other hand, felt like such a failure, not home much while they were alive and on that dreadful day, a defective dad. We didn't even live in this region of the United States, and so didn't come here often. As I recounted the last time we had come, the feelings of failure as a father rose to a crescendo and joined the crushing chorus of shame in my mind. Today, like before, we were coming to say goodbye. Again.

Of course, I knew they didn't hear us. Their own forced good-byes had already happened sixteen years before. We were the ones going away. Again.

This time, we were moving to Indonesia. We would be on the other side of the world, away from them. What kind of parents were we? What kind of a protecting father was I? Am I? The thoughts jabbed and hit me like cheap kidney shots delivered to a man who is already wounded and down.

As we continued to talk in hushed, reverent tones wiping our tears and stray leaves from the dark, black, stone marker, the sliding door of our vehicle opened. Elijah's face, with his dark, black hair filling the space where the door had been, was already transmitting to us what he wanted to do. He was asking if he could come and see where Caleb and Abigail were buried.

I was surprised. We had told the children to remain in the car. There was no real reason for them to see this place. They did not know the ones buried here. It was not a show, but a deep, personal scar for Penny and me to experience and try to heal alone. Yet, he wanted to see it. His face begged for permission as his mouth said the words.

I looked towards Penny to read her thoughts and she nodded weakly, so I said, "Okay, you can come." Confusion and prematurely short sentences seem to surround cemeteries.

In moments, Elijah, our vivacious, recently turned teenager, was there quietly looking at the gravestone. No one spoke. I did not know what to say. Maybe other men would have used the time to talk about really important things and lead their child into a time of growth, but not me. I was continuing to fail as a father and was lost in my own emotions.

There was more commotion in the vehicle as Hannah, less than eight months behind Elijah in age, took the time to unbuckle the others so they could see, too. After setting them free, Hannah helped our six-year-old, Noah, who in turn worked to guide and direct little toddling Hadassah, who eventually came as fast as her three-year-old legs could bring her.

Now, they were all with us. Four of them. One brown-skinned, three blond-haired.

To my horror they all began to walk on top of the grave place. They asked questions, seemed to touch everything. There was no reverence. No attempt to be quiet. It felt like they had no respect for the dead or the living.

I was overcome with a wave of frustration and anger. Didn't they know what this place was? How could they treat this like a park or a temporary break time from riding in the car? Sure, they were children, their questions were legitimate, this was new for them. But. . . didn't they realize the pain we were experiencing?

No.

How could they? Even adults fail to comprehend the nuanced distance between sympathy and empathy.

They began to ask questions about Caleb and Abigail's lives.

Memories.

Stories.

Stolen laughter.

Another wave of cascading tears.

My mind was nearly overcome with conflicted rage when something happened.

I can't really expect anyone to understand the full impact of that moment. Each of us knows there are certain times in our lives when things become very clear and we get a glimpse into something bigger, an overriding purpose that comes into focus and helps to recalibrate our perceptions of the past and the future. That happened for me, right then.

As the rage mounted and the emotions churned, a thought began to whisper, faintly at first, as if recently roused from sleep, until it became clearer and stronger in my mind. Then, it burst upon me like a trumpet blast!

There in that place, a quiet cemetery filled with reminders of death for untold thousands of people including my wife and me, I was witnessing life! Within inches of where our first two children were buried below, there were now four more walking around!

In a place of death, there was now life! Before, where we were broken shells of ourselves, God—and life—had given us four more children to love, to hold, and to experience life again! Absolutely amazing...

I experienced resurrection in that cemetery. How fitting!

A Word From the Author

⸙

This book is for anyone who has known the great pain of loss, great struggle, suffering, hitting rock bottom, regardless of whether you're a Jew, Christian, Muslim, Hindu, Buddhist, or follower of any other religion; whether you claim to know God or not.

I invite you to walk with me through Penny's and my story, through all of its twists and turns, pain and joy.

This story is about being human, about the fragile beauty of life, loss and love. We all have a different path and our journeys are not all the same. But our picture of God frames how we see the world and how we live our lives in it.

We all have ideas and questions regarding the character of God and the purpose of life. Those pictures may come from books, stories, family or preachers; they may even come from dreams or hopes of what could be. But we all have some sort of picture. Some of these ideas are positive, some ambivalent, some are even vehemently reactionary in regard to other peoples' or religions' pictures. I have screamed in pain and wrestled with questions. I have grasped for meaning, something substantial to hold onto. But God has held me through the deepest and darkest places. His mercy, love and faithfulness have been powerfully, unmistakably evident in my life.

In the pages and tears that follow, my prayer is that your own picture of God will be enlarged, that even amidst the pain or ashes in your own life you will find God's great goodness upholding you, and your life will be blessed. I pray that you will come to know a clearer, truer picture of Him, and you will see, as we have, a God whose faithfulness is truly, without question, undeniable.

Bryan C. Gallar

Undeniable

Part One

Devastation

Grief is a tidal wave that overtakes you,
smashes down upon you
with unimaginable force,
sweeps you up into its darkness,
where you tumble and crash
against unidentifiable surfaces,
only to be thrown out on an unknown beach,
bruised, reshaped.

Stephanie Ericsson

Change

Life belongs to the living,
and he who lives
must be prepared for changes.

Johann Wolfgang

Change is constant. As much as people don't like change, it is the one thing that stays the same. None of us stands still in life. We are constantly facing new circumstances. So it was for me.

In 1988, I chose to be a student volunteer teacher, going to the island of Chuuk (it was called Truk back then). With nearly one hundred other volunteers from various universities around the USA, I was brought to Hawaii for a few days to learn how to teach before heading to the respective islands scattered across the North Pacific. A noble idea that was! Bringing college students to Hawaii and expecting them to listen to lectures on teaching despite the sun, beaches and bikinis beckoning all thoughts elsewhere. But we were there, choosing to commit the next year of our lives to serving others. What a bright and beautiful change from college life, with promises of surf, snorkeling, and maybe even love. I don't remember learning any classroom-altering techniques from that week, but I know I had fun in Hawaii.

Almost immediately, I met Penny. We were still in Hawaii, still supposed to be learning how to teach and lead classrooms, and yet, within days, we had already gone on an excursion together. I am not sure either of us would have actually called it "a date." It seemed we had already mutually scanned the group of people going to our island and decided we were the most compatible for each other. Romantic? Maybe. Perhaps desperation on each of our parts? Looking back, we each had our reasons to look for "love," and we left Hawaii already interested in each other and contemplating a future together.

On the fantastic island of Chuuk we adjusted to our new routine as teachers, and life began to shift into high gear. Penny taught second grade. Picture thirty-two students crammed into a second-story room designed for twenty, with makeshift benches, holes in the floor, and a flimsy wall acting as referee in a shouting match between her classroom and the next (also overfilled). The school was regularly deafened by the protective tin roof which transformed a rain shower into another Pearl Harbor invasion of bombs and machine gun fire, causing education to cower in the corner. Noise, chaos, and ineffective teaching skills are mostly what Penny remembers. Hopefully her students gained something more than that.

I, on the other hand, had the elite group of eighth graders. Some of them were very bright. Others were very old yet still attending school for some reason I could not understand. One of them was only about one year younger than I was! Imagine an eighteen-year-old eighth grader! That was a first for me. I like to think that I did a good job teaching. I know I gravitated to the more advanced students, and they did well in their final examinations, with three of them being accepted into the best high school on the island (a record at that time).

There were nine teachers that year, two guys and seven ladies. So, the odds were good for me to be with Penny. Competition was low and the other American could have all the rest of the ladies if he wanted! There was a nice Filipino guy working nearby who wooed Penny's heart for awhile with his singing and guitar playing, but in the end my persistence paid off. Within three months Penny and I were engaged and later, in June of 1989, within a week of our return to the USA, we committed our lives to each other in marriage. The ceremony was performed in a courthouse, with later plans to have an event in August to include my family when they could come down from Alaska. Young and inexperienced, we were now married, going forward together into a life teaming with dysfunction, after a year of radical and rapid change.

It was not easy being married that young. We really didn't know each other in the "real" world. Living as volunteer teachers in an idyllic tropical island can cast a spell over you. We had met, dated, engaged, loved, walked hand-in-hand on sunset beaches, and married, all within ten months' time. We were two kids, twenty-one and twenty, now bound together. No job, no money, and many would say, no hope of a good future! But, we had love, right? So we thought. Love, by whatever definition we give it, always changes. It must change as it grows, or die.

We had conflicts of various sorts. Two broken people trying to make a go of life together. Someone once said that every marriage is six people getting married—the guy that I think I am, the guy that Penny thinks I am, and the guy down deep I really am (maybe even unknown to myself); joining up with the gal that I think she is, the gal she thinks she is, and then the one she really is (again probably unknown). Marriage, then, is the task of getting those six people to become one! That is not usually a peaceful endeavor. But, we began that process—ready, set, fight!

After some failed attempts trying to sell multi-level marketing health products—and even used cars—I finally began a life of selling books, door-to-door. Good books. Books about God and the Bible. I had always wanted to serve God, but I didn't have the self-control or patience to surrender to training, or the college degree to become a pastor. In fact, neither Penny nor I had finished school. So, this opportunity to meet people, touch lives, and give them good news seemed like a noble thing for me to do, and, quite frankly, was my only choice at the time! I enjoyed much of the work and learned many valuable lessons about people and God.

However, even with my commitment to serve God with all of my life, and a wife willing to follow her young husband into the unknown years ahead, it was not easy. I am not a naturally gifted salesman, so our first three years were very difficult. It was a time of long days, low pay, broken hopes, and regular experiences of failure punctuated by temporary miracles which were quickly replaced by feelings of uselessness in the grand scheme of life. It was hard; it left scars in our lives.

Every day was wrought with change. We seemed to have no ability to budget ourselves since all of my pay came from commissions. My schedule seemed driven both by habit and the necessity of hope for more income. Newlyweds are supposed to be in the honeymoon stage, united and facing the world together. But in our first year, we were more apart than together.

Penny wanted to trust me in ways that she had not felt God previously providing for or protecting her, and she felt like I wasn't doing much better. At home and at work I lived with a tangible feeling of failure. Within two years, my sales performance led us into bankruptcy, adding a ten year scar to our fledgling credit score. In the midst of those months and early years I believed that my value was based on my performance, and that performance was not adding up to much! So, there we were: two confused, immature kids making a mess of our lives.

Penny would stay at home, bored, waiting and wondering what I was doing during those ten to twelve hour days. Maybe she was praying, but more likely, not. Since her life journey up to that point had gone through some very dark places where she believed God had not proven to be particularly loving nor protective of her, she struggled with self-worth. Intellectually, she was committed to a label of faith, and we were regular churchgoers, but her walk with God was not vibrant. Her relationship between herself and God was, at best, wounded and, at worst, irrelevant. And, in light of her picture of herself, why would she even expect to have a husband who would care and provide for her? She regularly felt like this was all that she deserved!

When Penny miscarried within eighteen months of our getting married, she was devastated. Like a morbid metaphor, the death of our unborn baby gave birth to a seemingly endless life of hopelessness. As I tried to fix the pain that a man cannot understand, I suspect my actions cut her so deeply that her dreams of a compassionate husband died, as well.

My relationship with God, on the other hand, was broken in another way. On the outside I was strong, faithful, a model young person. But that facade was laced with bravado and pride. Knowing God, for me, was about knowing information or theology about God. Information about, and the ability to describe God, was my picture of faith. I have always been someone who learns quickly, and I had learned to prop up my self-worth by comparing myself with others. So, even while my salesmanship and income were both pathetic, at least my substantial Bible knowledge made me feel better and "more holy" than most. Because of this way of living, I had been ordained as a church elder at the age of twenty there on Chuuk! I took comfort in my own knowledgeable righteousness.

My faith was based in knowing how to describe God, defend theology, and argue my point to others (even if they didn't want to know). I acted like God was mine to contain, share, defend, and propagate. From many church members' perspective I was an "on-fire" young person, defending and sharing the faith to the untold "lost" people (or, simply others who were not in *my* church) whom I met from day to day. When I went to church or various meetings, I always had a powerful story or theological battle to relate, thereby encouraging others and, at the same time, making myself feel substantial and "holy." All the while, my pride masked a deep sense of worthlessness based upon my performance.

We were broken people with holes in our souls that marriage had no hope of fixing. It wasn't the life we would have chosen. People don't wake up and say, "hmmm, I want to feel hopeless and worthless today." Or, "I think I am better than everyone else, so how can I make sure they know it?" No, I think we simply fall into these traps of thinking, these pictures of life, of God, and of ourselves. We don't intentionally chart our life's course into tumultuous waters. It's more like waking up one day being lost at sea and not knowing how to get back on course, with each wave and storm pushing you further and further away from where you want to be.

Until something changes.

Decimation

Sometimes when you're
overwhelmed by a situation—
when you're in the darkest of darkness
—that's when your priorities are reordered.

Phoebe Snow

December 3, 1994, began like many other ordinary days before it. Penny and I awoke, prepared ourselves for a new day, and roused our two precious children, Caleb (three-and-a-half years old) and Abigail (ten-and-a-half months), from their secure slumber. We then began the adventure of trying to get food into two young and distracted children without taking too much time or making too much of a mess in the process. After the pushing and cajoling we finally loaded them and their paraphernalia into our 1984 Buick Skylark with its nice, leaking sunroof. We had gotten it from a "buy here, pay here" car lot since our previous bankruptcy limited our purchasing choices and vehicle options. We finished our breakfast and got ready by seven a.m. so we could drive the nearly two-and-a-half hours to a church in Almond, Wisconsin.

Both of us were twenty-six years old, and we had been married for nearly five-and-a-half years. Our rocky start had settled into a humdrum marriage. Penny and I had grown used to each other with our failures and generational faults; we were doing the best we could given the limitations our choices had made. I don't know if Penny or I would have said we were truly happy at that time. I sense we were both still so young and immature that we really didn't know how to be truly happy with one another, or alone with ourselves. All the repeated woundings had made happiness a temporary phenomena at best. Now, having young children further complicated the struggle to love and be loved.

After the miscarriage years before, we had tried to start over. Originally, I hadn't wanted children. In fact, from the beginning I told Penny that, and had even made it a prerequisite for our marriage way back when we lived on Chuuk. She had agreed at the time, but changed her mind later on after we were married. I did not like that she had changed her mind, and it was another source of conflict. So, in the midst of my being a financial failure as a husband, her fresh loss of a little one from a miscarriage, and my betrayal of emotional care in her time of need, she pressed more and more for a baby to love, trying to find joy somewhere. Finally her nagging for a baby had led to Caleb being born, and then later Abigail. We were grateful and, of course, we loved them as best we could. But sometimes the past conflict would reemerge.

Caleb was a mild-mannered, shy boy. Cute, blonde, slim, and loving. He was very easy to teach, almost dysfunctionally so. Even a cross look could bring him back into line. Abigail was more vibrant and expressive.

She loved hugs and food. She was a happy baby. Meal times were precious memories. Even though I had not wanted kids, my favorite experiences were coming home to our small, rented, mobile home and hearing Caleb yelling, "Daddy's home!" while running to the door with AbiJo, as Caleb called her, crawling behind him. Caleb and Abigail were blessing our lives and breathing fresh wind into our listless sails, even if I didn't know it.

That morning, however, as we traveled to the church, I distinctly remember fussing at Penny about something insignificant which clearly tainted our ride together to serve others. Funny how we can wound the ones closest to us all the while we're planning to be a blessing to relative strangers. Maybe it's easier to be loving to those you don't know. Or, perhaps it's more a sustainable show for short periods of time.

I regularly volunteered to speak in the little country churches, helping out various pastors who had districts with two or more groups. I was not a professional speaker. I was not a pastor. I simply sold Bible books door to door. I had stories of God's miracles, or at least, of people buying books so my family could eat. I always had a fresh supply of adventures, and that seemed to be enough for country churches to ask us to come and share. No college degree, no title, no training, just a willing story-teller. We normally enjoyed traveling as a family and visiting other churches to speak, but that morning, joy was clearly not riding in the car with us.

The little church was like many before it, kind and accommodating. Nothing in the architecture stands out in my memory. Just a country church inviting people to worship God on the weekends after a busy work week.

Resurrecting our smiles as we exited the car, we met the cheery door people stationed to greet anyone who came to their little gathering, and they led Penny, Caleb, and Abigail to the children's classes. I went on into where the adults met to begin getting to know this church from an outsider's perspective. Having grown up as a military brat moving from place to place, I seemed content being an outsider wherever I went. Kind of like a chameleon wondering where and what color was safe for the moment, willing to sit on the fringes and first watch before showing who I was that day, in that particular setting. Modern research calls me a "third culture kid" because of that, and I am reasonably comfortable with that distinction—though naturally, I often feel outside of that label as well!

I enjoyed the adult Bible study discussion. I don't remember if there was much arguing or not that day. But normally, if two or more were talking about God and the Bible, then arguing seemed to soon follow. I am not sure why the most beautiful subjects can sometimes bring out the ugliest parts of us, but that seems to often be the case! As the time passed, I observed a few areas of conflict, and some topics I could speak to in my sermon. Looking back, it seems rather prideful for a twenty-six year old to size up a church within moments, then preach God's words to people decades older and wiser! I guess small churches are grateful for someone simply willing to come, and maybe in the end, God delights in using the ignorant to bless others. Without degrees and titles, I was certainly an ignorant tool in His hands that day! The funny thing is, I was so young and inexperienced I didn't even realize the irony of ignorance in that moment!

That day I preached about Ebenezer. No, not Dickens' Scrooge. The Ebenezer from the Bible: a rock. The stone of God's helping us. The prophet Samuel had told the Israelites to erect one after a notable miracle. It was a simple sermon sharing how we should each have a stone, or stones, of remembrance of where God has led us, not limiting ourselves to the stories of bygone years and giants or pioneers of the faith, but our own personal stories of how and when God has shown up. Write it down, put it on a rock, hang it on the wall: remember them! That's it. We really have nothing to fear for the future if we will keep an active record of how God has worked in our lives in the past! That was my Ebenezer sermon. I had three points, three stories to illustrate from my life or from my reading and that was it. Nice. Cute. Simple. I believed the sermon. I shared it with conviction. Yes, God had clearly worked in my life and I wanted to invite others to remember the ways that He had worked in their own.

Sermon finished, we ate, and then loaded ourselves back into the car to return home. As I clicked in Caleb's buckle on his car seat he smiled and said, "It's cold, Daddy." I returned his smile, assured him that everything was fine, and felt a tangible sense of relief knowing my work for the day was done, and now I could relax. We prayed, thanked God for the work He had done there, and asked for protection as we traveled home.

But somewhere between Almond and Fall River, Wisconsin, something happened. Our nice prayers and sincere commitment all aside, our lives were about to be irrevocably changed. Little did I know that God had only just begun working that day in ways that I could never have imagined, nor chosen!

As we wound our way out of the little town, I put my chair back to relax a little bit in the car as my wife drove us on home. I don't know how quickly I fell asleep, but at some point obviously, I was no longer conscious of what was happening. Caleb and Abigail were also asleep in the back seat.

All of a sudden I awoke with a shock as I heard my wife scream.

I quickly jerked forward from my slightly reclined seat just in time to see two things—a look of absolute horror on my wife's face, and then another car passing us as our car veered off to the right-hand side of the freeway. Before I could offer any help, within a fraction of a second, the car rolled about three times at approximately sixty miles per hour down the embankment, side over side with the driver's side taking the first, full impact. I was on the inside of the car on the first roll. With each roll I seemed to hear a voice or an impression saying, "pull your head in," and I did. Time seemed to slow down inversely to the chaos rushing around me. Crushing sounds, a scream, shattering glass, a cold blast of outside air, all invaded my senses. Finally, a thud and silence. The car was stopped.

Was it a dream? A horrible dream? Had my afternoon nap created this macabre scene?

When the involuntary roller coaster ride ended, my head throbbed and my ankle ached but I was still conscious and aware of my surroundings. No, it was not a dream, no matter how hard I tried to make it one.

Sometimes unconsciousness is a mercy.

Like an eery silence after a storm passes, my ears began to focus again and I heard the engine still running, so I turned it off, somehow immediately remembering that gas can explode in situations like that. As I did that I saw my wife slumped over in her seat, not moving. Blood. Vomit. Her hair and face were matted and marred with indistinguishable fluids and pieces of glass mixed in as well, as all around her, the windows were all gone and the windshield was hanging in place by its lamination only. I tried my door; it was jammed. I was overcome by a tangible, sickening terror. Was my wife dead? I called her name. No movement. Then, I turned to see where my children were.

Turning my head to the left and feeling a tinge of pain in the process, I saw something I will never forget, though a thousand prayers have asked for amnesia! Looking to the back seat where my precious children were supposed to be, I was horrified with what met my eyes. Instead of sitting in her child seat securely locked in and safe from the crash, my little Abigail was hanging out the back window by the failed safety strap which had become a noose! The other side of the seat, where Caleb should have been, was empty. Where was my boy? An unspeakable horror invaded my world.

As grief and the utter devastation of the moment began crushing me, I felt an uncontrollable, fatherly instinct bursting forth from within me to get to my daughter's side to help her. My mind went into pure parental power mode. How could I get there fast enough? Would it be in time? The questions, the fear, the power, the urgency pushed me to a place where I cannot even remember what I did. Did I overpower the door? Did I go through the window? How did I get there? The emotions are so powerful I don't know how I got to her side. All I know is the torturous darkness of those emotions overcoming me for those fifteen seconds of activity. As I reached her and held her, removing her from the strap, my hands felt how limp and unresponsive she was. I had failed to arrive in time.

Now another horror raised its head. Where was Caleb? Holding my little daughter in my hands, nearly overcome by the hopelessness of the moment, I began to search for him. He had apparently been ejected from the vehicle. Frantically moving from side to side, grasping my daughter close to my chest, wishing with all of my being that I could impart some movement to her, I searched for Caleb. With each passing second the hopelessness grew. Finally, nearly one hundred feet away, I saw him lying motionless in the grass. I ran to him and gently placed Abigail next to him trying to see if he was okay. No response. No answer. His chest did not move. I was too late again.

I remember kissing Caleb on the forehead. I don't know why. Maybe I thought a father's kiss could do something. It didn't. There I was, surrounded with what used to be my family. Caleb and Abigail were laying in front of me, broken and unmoving. My wife encased in a crushed vehicle a few feet away. The mangled steel of our Buick now aptly described my world. I arose and stumbled in circles towards the void between my kids and my wife, screaming out, "God! Where are You?"

Within moments of my sermon, where were the rocks, where was my Ebenezer? All I saw was decimation!

Loss

*If you truly want to grow
as a person and learn,
you should realize that the universe
has enrolled you in the
graduate program of life,
called loss.*

Elisabeth Kübler-Ross

All at once I fell into a deep pit. I might be metaphorically speaking, but that does not lessen its reality. Each person may have different ways to describe the walls of this hope-defying place, but "heaviness" and "darkness" are constant words associated with this thing we call loss, or grief.

In my clouded mind at the time, I vaguely remember actions taking place around Penny and the car. A police officer came up to me and began asking a bunch of questions. My name, where did I live, identification, etc. He encouraged me to sit down, and I sat still even though everything within me wanted to run and do something else—anything. He kept asking me questions. At one point in my frustration, confusion and shock I blurted out, "I bet you are happy I am conscious so you can get all your answers!" I don't remember his response. I am sure he was much more experienced with people in shock than I was.

Then, the EMTs came and began to load me onto a straight board. I started yelling at them to leave me alone and go work on my kids. Even though in my heart I sensed they were gone, I could not imagine being the one these first responders would focus on. I was fine! I am the father, I am here to protect my family. Help my kids, my wife! But, all of my words failed to dissuade the valiant volunteers as they gently overcame me, strapped my neck down, and lifted me up. As they carried me to the waiting ambulance they inadvertently tilted me on the hill just enough so that I could see my suit coat over Caleb's face and a sweater over Abigail's. The cinematic symbolism suffocated me. Now my heart's knowledge was verified: my precious children were dead.

A wave of indescribable horror began crushing me. The doors shut me in. Each bump down the road reminded me that I could not move. I was a completely impotent father! Useless. Grief, failure, guilt and fear now overwhelmed me. What could I do?

Nothing.

They worked on stabilizing me and gently but intently deflected each question about my wife and children. They said, "everyone was being taken care of, don't worry."

Lies.

Lies meant to help, for sure, but they didn't. I don't blame the brave, nameless responders. Their only concern at the moment was keeping me focused on staying conscious until I could be seen by a doctor to determine if, in fact, I was okay. Maybe I was simply walking around with a neck fracture ready to literally snap at any moment. No, the focus was not on my family, I was the body in their care at that time. Their priority was to save my body, since nothing could obviously help my mind after what it had seen. Bandages, medicine, and operations could not touch my deepest injuries.

Upon arrival at a very small hospital, I was x-rayed and visited by the attending doctor who determined that I was not in any danger. My head and ankle were a little sore from being my pivot points in the car as it rolled side over side down the hill. But both of them are hard, and I was going to be fine.

Physically.

Then, the doctor had to do something I am sure none of them ever want to do. He had dedicated his life to saving lives, not destroying them. Apparently the nurses and first responders were not allowed to deliver the news. It was his tragic responsibility to tell me that my little Caleb and Abigail were pronounced dead at the scene of the accident. I would not be taking them home with me.

Never again. The finality of those words nearly finished me.

My wife!

What about my wife? My question resulted in a still, somber face staring intently at me. She was, even now, being transported to the medflight helicopter after being cut out from the car. That little hospital could not help her. Her only hope was miles away at the major trauma care hospital in Madison. If she survived the journey. . . . All I could hear was that minuscule but powerful word, *if*. If she survived, I could find her there. But that hospital was at least an hour away from me!

Another person came in at that time. The chaplain. He was the person who would try to work on my deepest injury. We talked a bit, and he did his best. But I was outside of his range of help then. So he prayed and in so doing, did all that was needed.

A nurse helped me find a phone, and I made what would be the first of many horrible calls in the hours ahead. I needed a ride to Madison. With that call, the horror of our afternoon invaded the lives of our friends. Within forty-five minutes my precious friends, Greg, Lesa and Debbie were with me as we raced to catch up with Penny. Tears, hugs, disbelief, and silence filled the minutes.

When we finally arrived at the major care unit, we were told that Penny had, in fact, survived. They didn't know how long she would be alive, and if, or how she might exist if she did live. They knew there was incredible head trauma, both of her lungs were collapsed, and there seemed to be some broken bones as well. She was intubated, medicated, and nearly in a coma. Now we had to wait to see if she would remain alive, or quietly slip into the same resting place as our precious babies. I looked upon the broken form of my wife in numbed disbelief.

What could I do? What could I say? She could not hear anyway. She might not even be cognizant of anything anymore. Her broken body might only be holding what used to be her mind. She might never come out of this. Maybe that would be a blessing since she would never know what had happened.

My world continued to be consumed with the new reality that everything had changed within a few moments. Whatever my life would become after this day, it would never be the same.

I stood for what seemed like hours staring at my wife. Her face was already nearly unrecognizable. The swelling had overtaken her features and turned them into one big mass beyond normal proportions. Her hair was matted and discolored and filled with glass and other debris. She had not been cleaned up. They simply tried to stabilize her first. The tubes and sounds of the machines helping her breathe added to the other-worldliness of this moment. No movement. Though she was technically alive, this was obviously not life. Disillusionment, prayer, questions, hopelessness, faith, all seemed to collide into a swirling vortex of forces beyond my control, and in their wake, devastated every part of what I thought I was.

What would happen if my wife died? I had already witnessed the death of my two children, was I about to be forced to watch the life drain out of my wife as well? What would life be like without a family? Where was God now? How could a good God allow so much pain? Have I believed a lie? Was my testimony of faith in the church only hours before just a collection of cute stories and Bible verses passed down through the ages that fail in the darkest of times when they are truly needed?

I was alone in the room and with my thoughts. Only immediate family could join me, and there was no one else there. I later learned my brother and grandparents were traveling through the night to arrive as quickly as possible. My parents were in Alaska desperately trying to arrange for the very first flight to the Lower 48. Penny's mother was frantically doing her best to bring herself to the side of her daughter as soon as she could. But it would be the next day before I saw any of them. In their place was our local "family." More than thirty of our friends were weeping and praying in the waiting room, wondering what would happen to me and to Penny, wondering if Penny would even survive the night and what would happen to me as I considered life without my children and possibly even my wife.

Then, one of the nurses came and spoke into the storm going on in my mind. She needed to tell me something very important and invited me out of Penny's room over to where my waiting friends were. As I turned to leave, after her continual assurances that there was nothing I could do and that everything that could be done was being done to help Penny, I was once again face-to-face with the reality of being completely useless. Walking away, the storm grew stronger as it fed off of the added emotions of uselessness and even betrayal. What kind of a man was I? Maybe it would be better if I had died also? Where was my God now?

There, in the company of the friends who brought me to the hospital and others who had joined them, the nurse looked very directly into my eyes and said that I needed to sleep. She told me there was nothing I could do, and that I needed to take care of myself. She was concerned not only for Penny, but also for me. Within one day, she said I would very possibly be feeling an incredible amount of physical pain given the stress and strain my body had just experienced, let alone going through the turmoil in my mind. So, she commanded me to sleep, and my dear friends created a plan so I would not be alone on that first hellish night.

Greg immediately volunteered and said that he would not leave my side and would stay with me as long as was needed. I nearly collapsed into his arms. The torrent of tears broke through, and I sobbed uncontrollably. My friends surrounded me and held me, crying freely. In their arms and support, slowly their collective love and faith pushed the hopelessness aside, temporarily. But in their eyes, lurking behind their tears, I saw fear. Like an uninvited guest in the room, interrupting everyone to ask the same questions, would that night be the death of my family and also my faith in a good God?

Eventually Greg pulled me away. We went to a nearby guest room and, with the help of medication, I was overcome by a fitful sleep.

Brokenness

I eventually woke up after the effects of the medicine wore off. Looking out the window I was disgusted by the sun's rays introducing December 4. My world had ceased to exist, but time just marched on, pausing for no one. The bitterness I felt rose like bile in my throat. Futility and finality framed my thoughts as I felt various places of pain in my body with each movement. Tangible reminders that this was no horrendous dream. Brokenness inside and out was my new reality.

I showered, trying to wash away what I had seen. The soap was powerless to remove the mental stain, the memory of my hands holding my own, dead daughter. Unlike the visions of blood and guilt that drove Lady Macbeth to wander in the night, my mark of failure and despair preparing to haunt me the rest of my days was in the light. Eventually my uncontrollable attempt to drown my world stopped and I dried off my tears.

I prayed. In my delirious moments before falling to sleep the previous night, I had also prayed. Why?

Why was I even praying? I was greatly confused about whoever and wherever God was at that moment. It made me wonder: why *do* we pray? What do we expect to come out of it? What is prayer?

My family and I had prayed less than twenty-four hours before to have a safe trip to our home and back, thanking God for the chance to serve and bless. How had that worked? My family was now split into three geographic locations: my children stone cold in some holding room awaiting the autopsy to determine the exact cause of death, to make sure that we had used the car seats correctly in case there was any reason for a wrongful death suit by the insurance or State; my wife connected to more machines than I had ever seen used on a person barely hanging onto life; and me, a walking, broken, useless father with no reason to return home. That prayer seemed like a colossal failure!

So, why pray? Did I envision God as some divine bell hop waiting to fulfill my every desire only to see that He can be capricious in His response? Some days, "yes," other times, "no?" Or, did I think that my prayers would be answered if I had enough faith? I'd heard those things and even read them in the Scriptures. So, was my lack of the proper amount of faith the problem—and therefore the reason—for my children's death and my wife's ongoing struggle to live? Was it my failure again? Did my "faith account" just not have enough in it to turn this devastation aside? Was this a huge bounced check in my bank account of life? Why didn't God just give me a loan? I would gladly have paid it back, into eternity, if necessary. Was God some unfeeling judge simply reading the verdict of the jury and dispensing punishment for my lack of faith? Do we pray because it's simply our culture and habit, a modern equivalent of the rabbit's foot of old? I did not know then. But, I prayed; hoping against hope that God would hear and then do something to help. But I did not even know what to ask. Should I have asked for Penny to be spared? What if she was mentally going to be irreparably incapacitated? What if the brain trauma was too severe and she would never be the person she was before? Did I even want her to live under circumstances like that? What a horrible question. What about me?

What did I *want*?

I wanted what I could not have. I wanted time to reverse and reset. But if so, how far back? Just to the last hug, or the sight of seeing Abigail take those first steps? Or, would I want to start the whole day over and try to be more loving to my wife? Or, maybe even further back to try and unwind the habitual dysfunction, or misplaced hours spent playing games on the computer in order to, instead, work on becoming a better father and husband? "What if" began to overtake my mind in a carousel of confusion. Ideas and scenarios moved up and down, some looking better than others, but ultimately going nowhere and changing nothing. Frustration, anger, fear and hopelessness moved prayer out of my consciousness and took residence. It would be many months before they would relinquish control of my mind.

I dressed.

I thanked Greg, who had stayed with me, and we prepared to go and see if my wife had survived the night. We stumbled out the door and headed towards the hospital. On the way he told me of phone calls of concern and prayer being received, and gave me an update on the travels of my family. Even now, my brother, sister and grandparents were waiting to hold me in the cafeteria, where we were heading. Did I want any food? Food? I guess that mattered. I wanted to see my family.

Moments later we were walking into the cafeteria and my eyes fell on my family. Though tired and with the marks of worry etched deeply on their faces, they sprang to my side ready to hold me. Greg seemed to disappear, knowing that I was now in their care, and they received the baton gently as I fell into their arms, weeping uncontrollably. My brother Jeff, two years younger, had always been the stronger one in our friendly-natured fights, and he literally held me up as the tears erupted and provided his first shower of the day after driving all night.

Grandma and Grandpa Freeman were faithfully standing there, full of love. Years ago they had taken both Jeff and me into their home when they really did not have to. Their son, Dean, had chosen to marry my mom, an older, previously divorced woman with two unruly four and six-year-old boys who had obviously been without a daddy for two years. Yet, he chose to take on the responsibility of a family, when he was only twenty-two years old, a mere sixteen years older than I was at the time he became my father! As I look back, I respect his amazing willingness and bravery in taking a chance on love, and on us.

My dad's choice stands as a reminder to the power of a life well-lived, and how our choices impact others in ways that we can never fully realize. But, beyond his choice to love both my mother and us boys, and in giving us a chance at a home again, Grandma and

Grandpa went beyond the nuclear family definition and fully accepted us into the greater Freeman clan without any reference to blood relations, or our past. They truly loved us and we knew it. We were part of their family, even without any genetic connections. That morning as they surrounded Jeff and me, it was fully descriptive of the love they had given us through the years.

Through my teary eyes I saw my seventeen-year-old sister, Stephanie, outside the circle sitting at a table crying, and trying to process a grief that denied comprehension. This tragic news had torn her from the festive December plans occurring at her school, and had thrown her life into turmoil and vicarious pain as she realized her oldest brother's family had just dissolved. At this critical time in her own life she was witnessing the decimation of my family, and it cut into her heart deeply. Though my pain did not allow me to realize this at the time, the death of my children would leave a scar on her life which would take years to work through.

Eventually the urge to cry subsided and we ate some food. After the awkward moments of eating and not knowing what to talk about, we all went up to see Penny. I already knew she had survived the night, but in what condition? The doctors were still keeping her unconscious for reasons I didn't understand. Apparently they did not want her struggling in any way during these critical hours as they waited for all the swelling to go down, or for her to . . . simply give up and die. No one talked about that.

Entering her room I was horrified to see my wife in her swollen condition. Once again the tubes, sounds and smells assaulted me. She had been cleaned up a little bit more, but the tragic reminders of our ordeal could still be seen in her matted hair. She did not know I was there. The others saw her momentarily, and then we all went into another room to wait for some explanations from the doctor.

Later that day Penny's mother, Anna, arrived and was taken up to see her daughter. When she turned into Penny's hospital room, she did not believe the person before her was her own daughter because the swelling was so pronounced. It had literally filled in all of Penny's facial indentions and enlarged her head so much that she was unrecognizable to her own mother! My family did their best to hold Anna in her pain. I had nothing to give anyone else. Anna wept freely as the tag team of loss battered at her heart: her first grandchildren gone, and her precious daughter on the brink of death.

The doctors did their best to console all of us, and tried to prepare us for the very real possibility of Penny having severe brain damage if (that nasty little word again) she actually survived. They let us know that soon they would take her out of the medically induced sleep to see what might actually happen. We waited.

A few more hours elapsed as we sat facing each other with hearts very full, yet having no words to say. Prayers were offered as more and more friends came, and they did their best to console us. We all cried together. The outpouring of cards, gifts and hugs actually began to overwhelm me. They were all a blessing, but eventually the numbness took over. The same questions, over and over, replaying the pain and loss; the same sincere words of care, comfort, and prayer trying to speak hope into my hopeless life.

Towards evening, my mom and dad arrived all the way from Anchorage, Alaska. Through the tireless work of the Red Cross they were able to change their existing flights and then make all the tight connections to traverse the thousands of miles to my side. They had actually been previously scheduled to come just one week later to see family: for Mom to see Abigail for the first time (Dad had seen her earlier in the year), and then for both of them to rejoice in my brother's wedding on the 18th of December. Now, everything had changed. No more grandchildren to play with and hold, and any hope of happiness for Jeff and AnneMarie's wedding would require divine grace and/or selective amnesia. Just seeing them broke the dam again. Tears enveloped us as we held each other.

Finally, the doctors said I could go in and see Penny and try to talk to her as the drugs should have worn away enough for her to begin to respond *if* there was going to be a response (I was beginning to hate that little word).

Quietly, Jeff and I went in. I could not go alone. I stood at my wife's side, afraid to hope, afraid to know whether she would ever speak again. We waited. Slowly I defied my fears and touched her right arm.

It moved!

Shocked, I began speaking to her, all the while bending closer to hear anything she might say. Hope temporarily struggled free from the stranglehold of despair. Could she actually be in there, still? Could my wife survive this terrible ordeal?

Time slowed. She seemed to know I was there and then slowly one eye opened as she began looking for me! A surge of hope pushed me forward. Jeff moved closer, supporting me, so I would not lean on her broken body.

There was no smile as her face could hardly move with all the swelling, but her eyes searched. She saw me!

My wife was in there somewhere. Slowly her mouth moved as she began to speak. My anticipation grew as she labored to find her breath with both lungs collapsed and on machines. I did not hear it at first so she whispered it again. My brave, precious Penny; what would she say? Her first words barely escaped, "Where . . . are . . . the . . . children?"

It seemed my whole world collapsed again. The momentary hope retreated before a crushing wave of despair and horror realizing that she *did not know!* Of course, no one could have told her. She had been unconscious. She was naturally being the loving mother she was, fighting to exist and care for her children. Her very first conscious thought was for her babies.

Oh, God! Why me?

Darkness pummeled me. What was I supposed to do? Do I dare tell her that they were gone and she would never hold them again? How could I? Where were the doctors now to do that job of telling her? Did the responsibility of telling her the worst news a mother could ever hear belong to me? Would I be responsible for taking away her hope of life? If she was told, the real possibility existed that she might lose whatever fight was left. Caleb and Abigail were her *life*. I certainly wasn't. All of my dysfunctions and failures had wounded her deeply through the years; I certainly could not be enough to fight for!

Futility, failure and finality framed me in. Hopelessness and despair pounced on me, kicking me, punching me, crushing the life out of me. My legs buckled, the brokenness bursting from within, and I could not stand. Jeff's arms tightened and held me up as the words escaped from my lips to Penny's ears, "they are gone, honey, they are dead."

Her eyes closed. She was silent. Brokenness descended on me like a captive locked away in the cell of hopelessness.

Goodbyes

There are no words to describe
the pain of burying a child,
and specifically there is no word
to label your new, lifelong status.
If you lose a spouse, you are a widow;
if you lose a parent, you are an orphan.
But what about when you lose a child?

Lisa Belkin

The rest of that week began to unfold, each moment moving me farther and farther away from our life before. Each interaction was a stark reminder of how everything had changed. Yes, I was surrounded by family and friends, yet all of the conversations were subdued by the loss of Caleb and Abigail, and the fear of losing Penny as well. Gone was the jovial laughter of family when they are together; tears became our shared unity. Church members began to pour out love and hospitality for my family in ways that can only be described as heavenly. Support came through food, gifts, places to stay, transportation, and most of all, simply being there and holding us when we needed to be held. I can remember very few words from that week, but my heart is filled with untold memories of their acts of love showered upon us. The old adage rings true again: actions speak louder than words.

Amazingly, Penny began to show enough signs of improvement and clarity in her thinking that the doctors adjusted their prognosis and expectations for her future. They began looking at her other non-life-threatening injuries. As the swelling seemed to dissipate and her consciousness grew, there were many times of talking and crying together. She would ask for details of the accident. I could not share them. They were too devastating for me, let alone for her to hear them right then. She wanted to know that she was a good mother. I could certainly affirm that. I asked her what had happened to cause the accident. She did not remember. She had no memory of any of it. In the years that have passed it seems that God mercifully allowed her to forget the torment of two days. What a gift; given to one, yet withheld from another. Why? For years I had felt cursed by the mental pain and flashbacks from the day of the accident, until I realized that I had been given a great trust. I was the keeper of the final memories of our children. Their smiles and laughter, Abigail's first steps, even their peaceful faces sleeping one last time in the car as we drove down the highway. One day, with those memories, I would be able to help us find closure. But that day would not come for a long time!

I asked her what she had felt or thought in her times of silence and darkness. The simplicity and clarity of her words startled me. Penny had no memories, but she related how she seemed to know that she had a choice to live or to die. In her brokenness, with the deep scar of terror covering the last moments, she had sensed the gravitational pull to simply stop trying and die. But, she didn't. She wouldn't! Not my Penny who stubbornly chose to fight for life! This broken woman refused to give up when it might have been easier to accept her plight and naturally die.

Just as my father's decision years ago to take on an entire family at such a young age had changed the trajectory of my life up to this very moment, Penny's choice to stubbornly refuse to die has molded every one of her moments since. Certainly, some choices are more valuable than others, yet their weight is often only seen in retrospect and reflection. Watching Penny fight to keep living even in the face of such loss and pain challenged me to be more intentional with my life as well. How many hours had I so flippantly wasted with useless endeavors? I began to realize just how important each choice can be.

Later on, my parents and my brother took me to a place that I had never given any thought to before. Sure, like everyone else I grew up with jokes or horror stories connected with funeral homes, but I did not really know what went on there. People my age don't think of death. In our early twenties we think about what we can get, do, be; how much fun can I have. We are invincible! Death is for old people. No, I had never given even a moment's thought to what might happen in a funeral home.

But Caleb and Abigail were not old. As the makers of the film, *Lord of the Rings*, reminded us in the haunting scene of a king losing his mind over the loss of his son, he cries out in an unearthly voice: "It is not natural for parents to bury their children!" The reality of that human anomaly broke into my world as we sat across from the funeral director. Being in that place made me feel betrayed, angry, and completely dumbfounded. Decisions had to be made about notices in the paper; where to bury our children; how to bury them; what kind of casket? All of this overwhelmed me. How much did we want to spend? Wait! "Want?" I didn't *want* any of this! One important detail to be worked out was when might Penny even be able to leave the hospital and attend the funeral. I was so grateful I was not alone working these things out. The details of death devastated me.

Looking back on that moment, however, I can now see something beautiful was happening. Obviously, this business offered a service to people. Sure, there were sales involved and costs to be negotiated, but this was very different from any sales encounter I had ever had. Mr. Jensen, the director, was so patient and caring. His work was not that of a sales function, but of a ministry. His demeanor spoke care and peace. He gently led us through the foreign world of death and walked with us, hand-in-hand, as we made some of the last decisions for our children.

In the cavernous darkness, he led us with a gentle light. He ministered to us! Later, we found out that he had even committed to driving our children after the funeral, at his expense, to their resting place nine hours away in Michigan. Amazingly, the magnitude of his kindness helped to mitigate some of my misery. Tragedies like ours don't grow people, they reveal people. Months later when my mind could think again, I realized just how deeply he had served us. My respect for his field and calling grew exponentially.

In the end, all of the details were worked out. Mr. Jensen suggested arranging Caleb and Abigail in such a way that they would be holding each other in one, simple casket. More than just the financial blessing of only one cost, it created a moving, final memory of Caleb's love and care for his little Abigail, as he protected her in his arms, waiting for the resurrection.

The next request caught me again. He asked for some nice clothes to be brought from our home that they could use in which to bury our precious children. That meant I needed to go back to the house and try to find something nice to use. The simplest thing such as putting on their clothes took on new meaning now. The thought of going back to the house horrified me.

Later, as Penny and I discussed which clothes would contain and express the finality of the moment, we wept again. We were faced with a decision of how we wanted our children to look in their casket. All of our previous challenges and distance in our relationship seemed like a foggy memory of another life, as we were now stumbling together through the valley of the shadow of death. The shared pain was forging our hearts together at the deepest levels.

We tried to discuss the funeral but would quickly become overwhelmed, and looked to others to lead. Family and dear friends stepped up to the need, and prepared for the event as soon as Penny was well enough to attend. Friends rallied to line up beautiful music and loving support for us in behalf of our precious little ones. Miraculously, having turned a corner as if in answer to the thousands of prayers going up, it looked as though Penny would be allowed to leave the hospital briefly for the funeral only one week later.

The night before the funeral, six days after our world had been destroyed, Penny and I went to see Caleb and Abigail to say our goodbyes in private. Though time continues to flow, it has been powerless to erode the memories of that night which have riveted themselves so deeply into my psyche.

I do not have the skills to paint for you a picture of what happened and what we saw. But, if I did, you would see a dismal scene. Certainly, black would be the pervading theme. It was not only a cold, dark evening in December, it was also a "dark night of the soul" kind of night. One that would overtake us for months to come. The various hues would play off each other in a suffocating vortex of fear with the only burst of color found by ripping your eyes away from the devastated couple in front of you and looking at the peripheral flowers and plants sent by supportive friends. Inescapably drawn back to the black hole of hopelessness, you would again see the weeping couple trying to hold the unbending shells of their children. The bright clothing subdued by the piercing, longing stares of a Mom and Dad searching the empty eyes of their lost children. There is no way the brush strokes could capture the pain and agony bursting forth in a torrent of tears. Streaked eyes can be put on canvass or paper, but their pain cannot be felt. Such would be the painting trying to capture what you might see. The work could very well be called *The Tortured Goodbye*. It was such a private, painful experience. In the end, I have only my words to try to express what happened.

We were escorted into a nicely furnished room and left alone. The lights were dimmed, yet intentional. The colors and carpet seemed almost inviting. I cannot say it was beautiful as that would deny the metaphysical ugliness of the place. But, it had obviously been prepared to be the very nicest that it could be, given its purpose. The furniture was respectful and solid as though designed to hold people with all the weight of both worlds on their shoulders. It seemed figurative of humanity's ultimate waiting room: each person entering and waiting to see the ones who had gone before, and wondering when their own time was to come. Or, like a momentary haven between the known storm of the past and the yet-unseen future.

I pushed us forward. Penny's defiance of death seemed complete, though not without cost. She was short of breath after her two chest tubes were newly removed; a sling over her left arm held it stationary so her broken shoulder blade could heal, and riding in a wheelchair since she did not have enough strength yet to walk. Most of the swelling had gone down, and only occasionally revealed still more glass and grit from her scalp and hair. Moving closer, she looked intently to the objects in front of us, our babies.

Our eyes blurred immediately as we saw their faces layered in makeup. Their unnatural expressions reminded us that we would not be hearing their voices. Each was wearing a hat to cover the cutting evidence of the autopsy: Caleb, an ironically playful ball cap; and Abigail, a cute, white bonnet. The uncontrollable urge to touch and hold them took over, but we were rebuffed. They were stiff, unresponsive. Like life-size dolls made to look like our children, they could not move. The clothes were known, the bodies were certainly those of our precious little ones, but *they* were not there anymore! The geyser of parental pain erupted as attempts to hold them resulted in our anguished cries surrendering the hope of ever feeling their hugs again. Tears and words burst forth beyond our control. Things we wished we would have said. Asking for forgiveness for letting them die. Crying out their names over and over. Memories. Regrets. Desperation. Grief took shape and enfolded us, smothering out the light and hope. Time and intensity seemed to merge, defying all limits to our pain. We wept uncontrollably.

Eventually, after a timeless void, our counselor and friend, Frank, came alongside us and cried with us. He had been meeting with Penny a few months before the children died, trying to help us grow together and deal with our marriage issues. Frank knew our babies, and had seen how much we loved them, even in our dysfunction. He held us and spoke quiet, gentle words of peace in the storm bursting all around us. Gently, he helped us identify the pain, give voice to the grief, and slowly to rise above the waves. He ministered to us, reminding us of a day of hope coming. Finally, knowing that Penny's strength was rapidly diminishing and she would need it again the next day to attend the funeral, he helped us leave the room of pain, and our children, behind.

The next day came too quickly. There is no way that my memory can do it justice. All the planning involved, the people taking part, the location, the parking, all of it, happened without my conscious awareness. I was barely functioning.

The actual program was beautiful, I am told. I remember the faces, the tears, the love, the music, and of course, the pain. The sight of that church is forever stained by the memory of the casket sitting in the front.

No longer was this church only a place of worship, it was a place of horrendous pain.

The outpouring of love and support was staggering. Hundreds of people came to show their love for us and to remember the precious lives of our little ones snuffed out too early. Friends from far away drove for days to show their love. Songs were chosen to evoke hope in the face of sadness. Words of comfort and promises of restoration were spoken in the face of pain. It was all a blur.

At one point in the program, I asked to speak. A space in time was made for me. With my brother Jeff at my side, we struggled up the steps to the podium. I wanted to say something to the hundreds of people there weeping with us. Whether it was faith or even bravado pushed forward by a wild expectation to share, I challenged the people to remain true to faith even in the face of this horrendous loss. Numerous times Jeff's arms stiffened to hold me as my legs were unwilling to support me while I spoke. With my broken voice reflecting my heart, I tried to say thank you and to especially exhort the young people there to live their lives on purpose, to remember Caleb and Abigail and not let their deaths be in vain. The tears derailed many sentences and stretched them to unnatural lengths, but I continued. Jeff held me. I could not look down at Penny or my family, knowing that seeing their faces would dissolve all of my resolve. I pressed on, speaking of a faith that I could not feel but only hoped might be true, and called everyone to consider their lives in light of eternity. Eventually the words stopped. We retreated back to our seats.

After the program ended, everyone filed by giving their condolences and hugs. We had to protect Penny from being hurt in the press of their love. Family stood guard and shielded her from many, only letting the very closest of friends enter to hold her and whisper into her ears. So many people were there and challenged by our tragedy. Our babies' deaths were impacting many, many more than just us. The day marched slowly on.

We all said our goodbyes.

Part Two

Darkness

There is no such thing
as darkness;
only a failure to see.

Malcolm Muggeridge

Night

*The depth of darkness
to which you can descend
and still live
is an exact measure of the height
to which you can aspire to reach.*

Pliny the Elder

Night. The time when darkness reigns. It is often the setting of horror movies, bedtime stories, acts of passion and pain. It is also the world in which dreams regularly take over, a place when the subconscious mind begins to play tricks and repaints reality for those who are temporarily in its grip. Nighttime can be escape, or it can be torment.

Our first night back home was horrendous. Having to return to the very house we had left only eight days before, a reasonably happy family of four, now, just Penny and me, the shell of a family. Though it was only a small rented trailer with used furniture and nothing of any true value, it was all we had. And now both our kids and even the car was gone! As we walked into that known place, all the memories began to pummel us like a water cannon driving us deeper and deeper into our despair, realizing that we would never hear Caleb running in the halls again. No more sights of little Abigail crawling around sticking everything possible into her ever-ready mouth. Our parental impulse to know where our children were and to guard what they were doing lay ready but dormant as there were no extra sounds. The silence was eerie.

Our precious friends and church members had come during the week and tried to prepare the house for our arrival. Some had cleaned the dishes, provided food in the refrigerator, and another had come to shovel the snow off the walkway. There was even a small group of brave souls who volunteered to go into the children's room, with tears in their eyes and loving hands, boxed up all of the toys and clothes until another day when we could eventually deal with those sights. We knew that we were loved and, unlike others who never go back, it was that love that gave us the courage to even consider returning home.

On that first night home another one of our dear friends would not let Penny and me suffer alone. We were so grateful. Taking herself away from her own family for a few nights, she ministered deeply to us. She came and volunteered to help Penny with her medical needs and to simply be there in the living room if we had any needs at all. Such simple, yet tremendous acts of love blessed us so many times as we look back.

The only way we could sleep after those first few weeks after the accident was with help. We either had to be medicated or become completely exhausted. The exhaustion came from uncontrolled bouts of crying or cycles of arguments. Neither of us had anything we could give to the other, and we both needed more than either could give! It seemed like we were both barely functioning and the stress just battered away at us. When the pills did not seem to work, the rounds of crying and arguing would take its toll on our emotions, and exhaustion would eventually lead us into the quietness of sleep.

Yet, that sleep was rarely good. Often there were shallow times when we were really neither awake nor asleep, yet our ears were still hearing everything around us. They would begin to play tricks on us. Fortunately, neither Penny nor I have ever watched horror movies or believed much about ghosts, trusting that the grave holds its victims tightly until the day of reckoning; so our minds were not fighting the added weight of cinematic horror when a door seemed to move or a sound could not be readily identified. We were spared that added trauma. But, the repeated impulse to go and see if the kids were okay would simply reopen the painful reality knowing that there was no one in their shared room anymore. Their beds were unused. After a subconscious ruse like that, it would take much time and many tears to get to sleep again.

Other times, our sleep would be broken by memories or dreams. One night later in the winter Penny bolted straight up from bed. With her pulse racing, breathing as heavily as she was able to with her lungs still compromised, she cried out, "Our kids are cold, they need me. My babies are cold!" In her desperate delirium she began pushing to get out of bed and fumbled with her good arm to start dressing. I tried to calm her and slow her down. All I could do was hold her, reminding her that she could not reach them. They were no longer with us in the house. When the reality woke her up, she collapsed knowing there was nothing she could do to help her children. They were dead and frozen, hours away from us in Michigan! I held her until the weeping subsided and the giants of powerlessness and pain pushed us back into the bed, making horrendous bed fellows. Eventually the muffled sobs relinquished hold and an exhausted attempt at sleep took over.

I experienced different kinds of dreams than Penny's. My dreams were not limited to the dark. They could come anytime with little or no warning. All of a sudden my mind would go into a flashback from what I had seen on that day when my world fell apart. Though I was not hurt physically in the accident, what my eyes saw and my heart felt cannot be measured on the pain scale. The trauma and devastation were registered deeply in my mind, and through these flashbacks I was forced to relive unspeakable emotions and fear.

Sometimes I would have a hint that it was about to happen: my arms might begin to shake. Then my head. If I was driving, I knew there was not much time before I would be out of control. I would swerve quickly to the side to find refuge on the shoulder, all the while praying that this time it would not be too bad. Then, as my emotions surged to the surface I would begin to hyperventilate, body shaking, mind running uncontrolled through the crevices and broken territory of my personal terror. Hopelessness, fear, loss, faces, blood, vomit, uselessness, metal, grass, casket, death, cold, stiff. . . . Like a giant emotional supercomputer compressing and analyzing pieces and pictures, trying to make sense of it all. Going faster and faster with no rhyme or reason, just out of control emotions and responses. Cold sweats.

I would writhe, twitch, cry out, weep with hardly an awareness of my surroundings. Then, with all my circuits overloaded, eventually the emergency shutdown was pulled and a catatonic state fell on me, mandating silence and exhaustion. No solutions. No respite from the pain. Nightmares set free from the night.

The first year they were terrifying. They came with little warning and deep, unutterable pain. Sometimes the flashbacks invaded the dead of night and I would launch myself out of bed to try to save my children this time—to not fail again. Penny would quickly try to talk me back into the bed as I tossed things to the side, mumbling senselessly about the kids or something else trying to hurt her. Eventually her calming words would invite me back to reality and the phantoms of my mind would slither away into the darkness to strike me another time. Grieving together, we seemed to take turns through those dark nights of the winter of our life.

Some nights when my wife would go to sleep early, after waiting awhile in the darkness, I would quietly rise and go to another room. I found that during the weeks and months of walking with Penny in her pain and tears, sometimes I was drawn to believe that I had to be strong to hold her up. So I would often ignore my feelings and try to push them away and not deal with them. I don't know if what I was doing was strange or unique to me or, if it was something more likely a gender issue, more of the way men deal with their emotions. In the end, it may simply be that we each just grieve differently. But there were nights, horrible nights, when I seemed drawn to call out the grief from within my heart, to express the pain that I held in during the day.

So I would go and get the pictures. Pictures our dear friends had taken for us. I didn't know if Penny knew where they were. It was kind of like my personal stash, hidden away. A stack of them showing people, flowers, faces, cards, gifts, and of course, Caleb and Abigail in the casket. All of them spoke love but little comfort. At first the tears would come immediately as I remembered the pain and memories associated with this group of pictures. Months later, however, like an addict needing more and more for the same affect, it would take longer for the tears to come. I would push through them already knowing the order, knowing what image would come next as I flipped each one over with my emotions ratcheting up more and more as I got farther and farther to the back of the stack, realizing I was about to see my little Caleb and Abigail. As my finger finally slipped to that picture where I saw the peaceful, unmoving faces of my two children, then the tears would begin to pour. I wept alone without anyone else to witness, and especially not Penny, in order to not cause her more pain.

Other times, as a man, the tears seemed deeper down than before so I would turn to different pictures. Not pictures from the funeral, but the few that we had as we saw Caleb and Abigail growing up. Their smiling faces brought complex emotions to the surface. I never knew exactly which ones would erupt on any given night. There would be joy at seeing them again, if only in a picture, and my mind would replay loving memories. Yet each picture reminded me of my day-to-day faults as a father, and even on the day they died, my failure to save them. Other times, a deep bitterness would surface. I would struggle not only with my grief at their loss, but I would wrestle with the anger of being robbed of their company. The experiences we would never have with them. How I would never watch Caleb play baseball or walk my little Abigail down the aisle on her wedding day. My bitterness would turn to blame and my anger would lash out at God. Not only had I failed my children but God had failed all of us! Trying to hold back my screams of anger my hot tears would finally explode from deep within.

On the most difficult nights when I could not sleep, and the normal retinue of pictures had lost their affect, I would finally turn to the mangled picture of our Buick from the accident, or read the police report describing the event, and force myself to release the pain. Like piercing a can bloated with botulism, my body would retch and burst in the cathartic crucible of pain. For many minutes I would deal with wave after wave of agony and loss, letting the pain of weeks come out in one horrendous geyser. Eventually, the self-inflicted torture would release me to sleep.

Such were the many very dark nights.

Emptiness

Death is not the greatest loss in life. The greatest loss is what dies inside us while we live.

Norman Cousins

One day I was wandering in Walmart and I happened to be walking in one of the large aisles in between sections. I was looking around at my surroundings, watching people, and simply noticing things. I don't remember if I had a particular mission, or even a shopping list. I don't remember where Penny was right then. Maybe she was at one of the regular follow-up visits to the doctors working to get her lung capacity back to normal, or a physical therapy session trying to increase the range of her wounded shoulder while learning to cope with the loss of the use of her left hand and destined to live the rest of her life handicapped to one.

I don't remember what it was, but I was just there in the store, alone. Very alone it turns out, with only my thoughts for comfort and company. They were neither.

Each step moved me in and out of aisles and shoppers. I glanced at the people who had a purpose for being there, people who still had lives worth living. My steps slowed, my thoughts deepened.

Ever since our fateful day in December we were slowly becoming more and more aware of just how much our lives had changed. It would ultimately take months to realize what had disappeared in a moment with the death of our children.

Imagine.

One day we were a family of four. Car seats. Diaper bags. Always wondering and being on the watch for where our children were. People treating you like a growing family. Then, within hours they were gone.

All gone.

The replacement car was more empty. Getting ready to go out was much easier. No extra bags. No vomit-stained clothing. Just the two of us.

By the age of twenty-six we had been married five years, had had two children, and buried two children! People would look upon us as a young couple with no children now and never imagine or know who we were. Most of our friends all had children, but now we were wounded outcasts trying to find our place. In the wake of that tragic day our whole identity had been reset and socially erased.

Even the simple act of shopping was changed in our lives. We no longer had large lists of the parental paraphernalia needed in caring for children. We had no more need for diapers or wipes or cute clothes caught on sale. No, there was no more excitement at finding something small which would bring a squeal of joy or a twinkle to the eye of our precious little ones. No. It had all changed.

Not much need for food either. We did not eat a lot at home as our table had been transformed into a living reminder of the silence of death: no more food fights or childish chatter and two sides of the table were always empty! The remaining two seats were filled with two broken people eating out of need, not because we wanted to. So, with most of the purpose and joy of shopping gone, it became a function.

And as a function, sometimes it was therapeutic for the simple fact that it got us out of our home—no, not a home, it was a house. Our home was gone. We could get out of a house where everything was quiet and nothing but a horrendous reminder of our empty lives. Shopping could be a distraction. Anything to change the scenery and search for something on sale that could attempt to soothe the brokenness.

But even that function failed. Nothing worked for very long. Monetary purchases cannot replace those you love. They cannot bring your former life back. We had brief moments of happiness and stolen laughter when we would buy something for each other, but it was temporary at best. We lived with a tangible feeling of guilt for still being alive, and laughter seemed disrespectful to our children. So, whatever joy that emerged momentarily would be followed by regret, sadness, and a strange sense of betrayal.

Living survivors carry a beguiling guilt of broken camaraderie with those who are gone. How could we express happiness, even fleeting, when they were not with us? Shopping had changed. Its function was one more reminder of our traumatic life, walking in the shadows of death.

Even the process of simply eating in restaurants had been transformed. With our own table being a place of torment, we regularly ate elsewhere. But as we did, we would be ambushed again.

Stepping into restaurants to find nourishment and another distraction from our emptiness, the presence of families tore at us. Each table for four, each high chair, each sippy cup snapped into focus and screamed. But more than those symbolic visuals, our ears would immediately begin to hear everyone's children in the whole room. Not ours, but theirs!

The amazing power of the parental ear does not switch off when your children no longer make any noise. Audible assaults abused us. We still heard the muffled sounds children make. Their innocent laughter taunted and slapped us. Each cry for mommy and daddy knifed us to the quick. The repeated calls to get busy parents' attention were like Chinese water torture: slowly but surely driving us out of our minds wishing we could shake the parents and tell them to cherish each moment. But they wouldn't understand that look of pain in our eyes. We knew our children were dead, but we still wilted with each whimper, longing to bring care. The fading memories of standing at the door of our child's room breathlessly listening to catch the faintest evidence of their moving chest mocked us as we saw another woman's child peacefully nestled in her arms: dejectedly, our arms fell lifelessly to our sides as we relinquished another memory.

There were times when we simply could not handle it and would turn and leave. The cacophony of voices pelted the back of our heads as we mumbled some lame excuse as to why we were leaving. Further attempts to explain would only bring empty faces and awkward words. We would retreat to the forced silence of an empty car and weep. Eventually hunger would surface and drive-thru's became the solitary solace for the suffering. Such were some of the changes in our new world.

As I walked through that Walmart, I pondered those things. I was wallowing in the emptiness, and experienced the ironic loneliness of wounded people: surrounded by many, yet totally alone. Absorbed in my thoughts, I was not prepared for what I was about to face. Like a trained assassin waiting for exactly the right time and only one strike needed, one of the deepest wounds from the accident was about to resurface and pounce on me. This was the pain no x-ray could determine and no medication could touch.

Rounding one section I saw a child standing up in her shopping cart. Not in the large bin area where it is reasonably safe, but up in the front section designed for sitting, with the straps. This little child was not sitting. She was standing and rocking back and forth calling to her parent somewhere outside of my vision. Rocking, swaying, calling, and yet I could not see any parent near.

Immediately I was overcome with an inexplicable horror. Like a flashback I was momentarily seeing *my child* about to fall and hurt themselves. Fear and darkness encircled my vision as a train of powerlessness barreled toward me screeching its impending collision. All I could see before me was pain and death again, and what could I do? I was too far away to help. With just one miscalculation or bump that precious child would fall head first to the concrete floor below causing serious damage. Rationality stepped aside in the face of those feelings. I could not fail again. I must save "my" child. The face was blurry now as I did not know if I was in reality or in a flashback come alive. I began to walk closer to the child. I did not run because it would scare her, but I moved intently and quickly. I frantically looked to see where the parent was, but I could not see them. Who in their right mind would let their child do that? Don't they realize how quickly everything can change? Judgment and anger began to rise.

No parent! Where were they?

I was alone within sight of this potential doom. I got closer and closer until finally I was within range where if the child fell I could at least leap fully stretched and catch her head before it cracked on the unforgiving floor. Whatever pain I might experience would be inconsequential. I must not fail. I am sure my face displayed all the intensity and intention driving me.

Just then, from an unseen place on the periphery, the parent emerged and surveyed the situation. My face. My focus. My close proximity to her child! Her eyes began to transmit a look that I cannot bear, even now. All she could see was someone close enough to do harm to her child! Maybe a pervert or a child molester ready to prey upon her innocent loved one. Ironically using Walmart as the place to steal them away and then put their picture up on the board of missing children! There I was, close enough to reach her precious child!

Yes, her piercing, violent eyes were justified. With my mind I understood, but she could not see my heart. She did not know the torment that was raging within me, the good will I was attempting to do. No, I was not there to cause pain, only to help. But she could not see that. Her face flashed all of that judgment, and like a mother bear with her cub, glared at me to back away.

Of course I did.

Not only was I unable to help, but I had been relegated to the lowest level of humanity while attempting to do good. Her judgments and the perceived glances of the crowd now came into my vision and seemed to surround me. Guilt, despair, worthlessness, evil, impotence, outsider, disgust—each word and feeling took life, kicked at me, and drove me away, like a hero rushing to set a captive free from the oncoming train only to see the captive snatched away in the last moment and then the hero identified as the perpetrator of the dastardly deed and tied in their place to be destroyed, bearing the shame, pain and ultimately, death. I limped away, avoiding stares and hoping no security would accost me.

What an empty failure, again.

Grief

If you're going through hell,
keep going.

Winston Churchill

Some may ask, how do you get out of a pit like this? How do you deal with the overwhelming grief of death? How is it even possible to write a book such as this? I don't think there are easy answers. Given the fact that grief is a phenomena all will face, much research has been done regarding grief. But the reality is, it is beyond us to contain it!

I cannot imagine someone flippantly giving a recipe to deal with grief with all the ingredients detailed, or outlining the steps of grief like they would assemble a new desk, carefully glancing at the directions to make sure all the parts are used correctly and in order like this: first you go through anger, then denial of what has happened, soon to be overwhelmed with a long depression with times of bargaining and attempting to move your life forward until finally, *voilá*, you have acceptance! No, it is much more messy, more personal, like each unique fingerprint sharing certain identifiable parts with all the rest: all different, yet all similar. The outlined stages of grief according to one author may not be as crisply delineated in the research of another. Add to that the complexities of circumstance, emotional readiness, personality, and physical vitality, and you have a matrix beyond our full comprehension. Such is the devastating mystery of grief.

So it was for us. The months that followed the accident had forever altered the course of our lives. The darkness was beyond our human experience and I can only reflect and see these things in retrospect. In the midst of the storm, there is very little light and even less hope that you will survive.

Yet, though the storm was overwhelming both of us, each of us grieved differently. The way Penny dealt with things was distinct from how I dealt with them. As a mother, and a woman, she felt things in ways that I was incapable of fully entering. Yes, we walked together in the pain but we were also torn apart in other ways. We each needed to go through it on our own as well as together. Although grief seems to defy us at each turn while our emotions toss us from one wave of pain to another, I do see a way of describing it. I seem to see it more in extended metaphors.

Some of these metaphors could display some aspects of intention and process that maybe our resolve and personal choices might help; yet, another seems almost outside of ourselves, as though something or someone is sustaining it, and acts upon us and within us. I think those who have grieved have experienced both types in one way or another, and those who have survived have little room for pride in how they did it. Maybe we don't have many "how-to" courses because one seldom boasts of victory over grief. Death seems to run hand in hand with humility. It is the definitive equalizer of humanity! So these reflections are simply my way of trying to help explain what I felt.

The first metaphor is like a long war with soldiers battling through the months and years with victories, losses, casualties, amputations, and charges. There are short-lived moments of rest followed by waves of desperation and frantic activity in an attempt to simply stay alive. The fight to literally wake up each morning is the ongoing victory—life in the face of death. The intense desire to roll up into a ball and weep at the carnage all around us at times keeps us from losing our minds. Yet, after that desperate act of fighting to stay alive, choosing to try to continue *just one more day* while being besieged by hopelessness is another battle won. We press forward in the stubborn belief that we can survive, only to go through it all over again.

Ultimately the direction of the war is measured by those moments of choice to persist and push into the unknown. Yet, the relentless skirmishes batter away at all we know ourselves to be, and in the end, we are changed. With each loss, death lives. Life dies. At the end of the war to protect our lives, we see that our lives are no longer there: we have become something else. Whatever remains can only be the shell of what we were. And yet that shell has learned to function and exist one moment at a time in persistence and clarity. The will to fight has brought life from death.

The trained tenacity presses on like amputees stepping out into the bright light outside of the hospital with the aide of a crutch or prosthesis, mustering the courage to carefully and painfully amble forward to whatever is next. So the shell of who we were still lived.

Or, like the ships of war and devastation resting serenely on the ocean floor, evidences of battles lost, we become the infrastructure needed to house the most magnificent corals teeming with undersea life. Something comes from the brokenness. The shell of what we used to be can eventually be filled in with something new. War destroys. War also creates. The new "us" sees things differently, and feels life in ways unknown before.

We have a choice in how we react. The first metaphor allows for process, help and hard work to show its value so that in the end we will not stall in one of the many stages of grief and never fully go on in life again. Within this metaphor, Penny and I were greatly blessed by Frank and friends who helped us push through this war. We also found great value in various books which helped us navigate and make the choices needed to "win" the battle and accept our new life.

But the other metaphor is different. It is like a wild animal clawing away to extricate itself out from a pit deeper than it can climb. By no choice of its own it finds itself trapped, with little hope of life. With each lunge and stretch, energy seems wasted on the unforgiving walls. The heart pounds, the lungs cry out, muscles tighten and contract, and it seems the harder the animal tries, the more it fails. The higher it jumps, the farther it falls back. Sometimes a ledge may be found, but not enough to hold the weight. Crash, again and again, pain punctuated by failure. The dark cloud of dirt and rocks fall down upon the poor hapless being, blanketing it like the obvious despair gripping its heart.

The escape attempts are feverish at first and then less so. Eventually there seems to be a resignation to the reality of never getting out of the pit. Hopelessness seems to overshadow the one living. Despair takes residence.

But, then, like an unforeseen earthquake, something stirs and the animal claws again. It fights, jumps, hits the wall over and over again. Like a mythical beast that will not die, it struggles day in and day out just to survive, and as it does, *something* does happen.

The rocks and dirt from each attempted escape lunge begin to accumulate at the bottom, and eventually (in what may seem like a time-defying eternity), the distance to the top becomes closer than before. Standing on the newly attained height, the cycle repeats. Desperation, hopelessness, discouragement, almost losing hope. ALMOST. More deliberate movement, more accumulation, until finally, hope is glimpsed at the edge of the pit, and an emaciated animal hangs on, ready for another day to try living again.

In the months that followed the accident I experienced both of these metaphors. I can identify with the soldiers battling to go on, sometimes blindly stumbling into the next foray. With each volley of emotion and change I have felt hopelessness and despair literally wringing life out of me to the point that I have feared dying myself. I cherished those brief moments of hope which pierced the darkness, only to have them smothered by new barrages of mangled memories and dashed dreams. As the pain, confusion and weeping drained my very life away, I simply felt the need to collapse and die. Then, when hope was gone, mysteriously, something stirred from a place that I cannot explain nor control. Something bigger than I could ever identify began pulling me forward, moving me to try to get up, just one more time.

As Penny and I were thrust into our new world with grief as our captor, we struggled and fought to simply survive. Sometimes the battles were obvious and outside of us. Other times they were between us. Some days, the act of simply getting out of bed was revolutionary.

I noticed changes in my personality and memory. Before the accident I was a gung-ho, happy person. Afterwards I was subdued and felt guilty if laughter escaped. It seemed like a denial of our children's lives, and of losing them. It literally felt like part of me died that day as well, even though I was still walking around living. The happy-go-lucky, sanguine, extrovert was changing. Other times it was my memory. I was amazed that we could be traveling down the road and have an idea come into my mind such as going to visit someone, and I'd share it with Penny. Then, within minutes after exiting the freeway to go and see that person, I would arrive at a stop sign and no longer remember where we were going! It was crazy. We both seemed to lose short-term memory, and in the years to come even realized we had lost some long-term ones as well. Whole segments of our life were gone. The effects of grief on the mind are tremendous.

Sometimes I would be doing pretty well, thinking I was licking this grief, and moving ahead in the process. Then, from the corner of my eye as I drove through town I saw a familiar restaurant being renovated. Inside it had been a simple little ball pit where I had played with Caleb and Abigail when it was Daddy's time to watch them. I would buy an orange juice so I could be a customer and use the warm play place away from the Wisconsin cold. Recounting Caleb's laughter as we threw balls at each other brought a slight grin to my face. The joy of seeing Abigail falling into the balls backward and looking into my eyes for assurance that it was okay deepened my smile and took me back to that happy place and time. But now, there in front of me, the workers were filling it in to change the dining area. Under a new name and management the pit was no longer needed. Simply obeying directions, the workers were clueless that their actions were robbing me of that sacred space. Without warning, I was thrown into a time of depression lasting for weeks as another tightly held memory was torn from my life.

Some days we had nothing to give, nothing for each other and certainly not for anyone else. We would bargain with life, asking for the second coming of the Messiah to happen soon so we could see our children again. We tried to keep busy but no matter how fast we ran, the grief was faster. We could not escape.

It was as though we were locked in a hall of despair. Locked into an ongoing party of death. Forced to remain, we danced many times with denial. Spinning and turning away from the raw facts of our loss, trying to deny the song the orchestra had given us. With each repeated refrain we became more and more exhausted and angered. When would the next song begin? Finally, the dodging would stop and we would seek a momentary rest amidst the never-ending songs of hopelessness. With the notes echoing throughout the chamber and darkness the motif, depression would silently slip its hand into our pockets to steal away our most cherished possessions— our memories. As time went on our storehouse of riches diminished. Each day we awoke it seemed we could not remember Caleb and Abigail's faces as well as the day before. Their laughter and smiles were being drowned out in the incessant drumming of despair. Then anger would respond, charging in and assaulting all who were near, tearing away in frustration, trying to go back to the land and time of hope. But nothing worked. The music would get louder and the crowd of reality would beat us back until we would simply bargain for a slight stay of pain and try again. Then, the dance would begin all over again. The cycle seemed to be never-ending and hope had long ago left the room.

So we cycled. Over and over again. Anger. Depression. Bargaining. Denial.

As the fog of time lifted and the weeks moved on into months, we pushed ourselves to start over. Fighting, choosing, losing hope, getting up again, falling, and simply crying out one prayer:

> *Oh God, if you are there,*
> *please don't let both of us*
> *be at the extreme bottom*
> *at the same time,*
> *or we might never get up again!*

God heard us.

Stars

The darker the night,
the brighter the stars,
the deeper the grief,
the closer is God!

Fyodor Dostoyevsky

Even in the darkest nights, there are stars. Because of clouds, or pain, or even a refusal to look, though we do not acknowledge them, they continue to shine.

So it was for Penny and me during this horrendous time of darkness. Every now and then we could see a pinpoint of light bursting through the unspeakable void. Like a search party passing near us while we were locked away in that dungeon of grief, a brief light would awaken us to the possibility of hope, that a new day would soon follow.

The first "stars" on the horizon were the physical acts of kindness and presence of friends peeking into our chasm of pain. Realistically, we did not even know these human stars were shining at the time, but it does not negate their light. I remember the thirty or forty people who crowded into the hospital waiting room to hold me and cry with me on that cold December evening. I remember Denny traveling all the way back home just to give me something I had asked for in passing. Or, the loving way Darry and Ginny hosted my extended family during that week when I was helpless. In addition to that support, there were many loving hands and hearts who delivered hot meals to our house after the funeral. They realized that in our grief we might forget to eat, let alone think far enough ahead to plan to cook it. Their kindness continued for weeks and reminded us that we were not forgotten.

There were friends who came to help Penny clean and cook as she learned how to function with only one hand. Or, the sacrifice of the ladies who took her to the many doctor appointments when I could not. In our numbness we, unfortunately, failed to thank each of them. Yet each act shone brightly behind the clouds of our despair. They understood that they would not stop loving us when we were not able to thank them. They shone like stars anyway. Their light was seen and recognized!

Our little circle of friends seemed to know that of all the meals we would face alone, the one after church would be the most painful. That weekly time of rest and worship, when everyone was gathered and celebrating being a family of faith, was, for us, now alone, a mockery and torture. So, without any planning that we were aware of, the church rallied around us. Not for a month, or even three, but for a complete YEAR, we did not have to suffer being alone on that day of worship!

Amazing.

Curiously enough, the one timeframe that is not marked by any celestial luminaries became a different point of light for us. Each week when we came to church, someone would find us afterwards and invite us to eat with them. Opening their home to us and sharing the warmth of their love and food provided nourishment for both our bodies and souls. We still had plenty of time to hurt through the meals on the other six days of the week, and it left its scars. But knowing that there might be fellowship and kindness on the seventh day gave us hope. With so many participating in fellowship toward us throughout the year, their collective love was like a favorite constellation marking the path forward.

Other lights were more subtle. Not everyone would even know they were lights, but we saw them. Like the greeting cards that would arrive on each and every holiday for years after the accident. Knowing instinctively that holidays are family times and that ours was destroyed, one precious lady, Sharon, was faithful in remembering. She sent simple, hand-picked cards reminding us that we were not alone and that she was remembering and praying for us. On the birthdays that would have otherwise passed unnoticed, she remembered Caleb and Abigail. She was not afraid to cry with us, remind us, and to actively fight against the specter of forgetting. Seeing their names written with love on her cards denied the lie that the memories of our children were gone. Her forethought and care involved in such an act exponentially surpassed the monetary value of any card. The brightness and consistency of her light helped lead us into our new life in the months ahead. She will never truly know the power of her tangible love.

Stars like Sharon's transformed our night regularly for years to come. Some stars simply twinkled for brief moments, but their impact cannot be forgotten or lessened. One day in church we were sitting in the back near the section which had been set aside for families. I guess the habit of sitting back there had not died as quickly as our children, or we were just trying to physically deny our loneliness. For whatever reason, we were there. It happened to be the time for the children's story. I don't remember the actual story, but the children all moved forward to the front to listen. The themes of these short stories usually involved protection by the random intervention of an unseen angel or some other miracle. Regardless of the overriding facts, they always seemed to end well in those short segments. (It seemed a little inappropriate in reflecting back. Apparently we are supposed to let life break the bad news to the kids later on that life doesn't always end well, hoping they won't lose their faith when tragedy skews the "Rest of the Story" with a punchline no one wants to hear.)

As the drama continued to unfold and the miracle of God's protection became clear, there was a muffled sound in the back of the church. We were weeping. We tried to cover it up, but we were failing. Life's contrasts were wounding us again: no angel had come for our little children to set them safely on the hillside! The story had not ended well for them. The agony of divine betrayal was attacking us—in church of all places—and we could not contain the tears. Unable to leave, all we could do was try to cry quietly.

Without our realizing it, and without the story-teller even pausing, three precious ladies simply got up from their seats and walked across the church to sit with us. They broke the culture of arms' length piety and surrounded us. Squeezing into the pews to hold us tightly, they acknowledged the pain of loss. Like modern messiahs bringing comfort with their presence, they wept. Their shared sorrow fought back the cloud of depression that could have set us back weeks. Their arms and tears transformed the day. Stars like that remind us that if light is present, light wins!

Other events are so amazing that they defy mathematical odds. Like the precise trail of a comet splitting the night sky right on time, some phenomena cannot be labeled as simply coincidence. They hint at a law or a history that is much deeper than our experimental knowledge can explain. One such reality blazed through our darkest time immediately after the accident when we were forced to acknowledge God's love even as the children died.

The story came out a few days after the accident which still overwhelms my heart when I think of it. Even now I am moved to tears as I type it out. On that fateful day as I was in shock, oblivious to my surroundings and assuming everyone was dead, someone else had been at the accident site stabilizing my wife. A woman in a car behind us had witnessed the accident and immediately went to help Penny, holding her neck, and caring for her so that she could survive until more help arrived. But, she was not just any woman. The first person on the scene was a critical care nurse, literally on her way to work her shift that night at the only major trauma care hospital in that region, nearly seventy miles away! She actually worked at the exact hospital that Penny was later taken to by helicopter! Out in the middle of nowhere Wisconsin, with only volunteer first responders in the county, God had literally coalesced time and space to have this experienced and compassionate professional on hand immediately!

Absolutely amazing!

Days later when she came to see Penny in the hospital, she told us what had happened. As the details were shared about her being at the right place at exactly the point of need, light seemed to explode into the darkest time of night and produced a tail of hope that we could hang on to and remember for years to come. It defied coincidence and shouted "miracle." Just as the tales of some comets are the subjects of lore in many countries, so her story proclaimed grace in the face of death. It was an event that could not be ignored and remained as a testament of God's undeniable faithfulness to us in the darkest months ahead.

Another function of the night lights are to display the changing of seasons. Whether we like it or not, life has its seasons as well. We may deny them, we may curse them, but they come regardless. If we are wise we will learn to embrace them. Some stars can only be seen in the fall and winter. The irony of those stars' timing invokes hope while grass, ground, and trees show the colors of death.

Ed and Joy helped us to see the change of our life season, and in their love and wisdom, gave us the needed preparation to survive. It took a bold and rarely seen love to do what they did.

One evening they came alone to our home. We did not realize it then, but they must have intentionally planned to leave their child with someone else. I don't remember how long we had known them, but our Caleb had played with their daughter and were nearly the same age. With their second child about to be born soon, we had laughed, shared similar parental challenges, and had grown close. Having them visit brought joy to our otherwise hurting hearts.

As we talked a bit and caught up on the latest activities, they noticeably shifted their focus to us. I still remember it vividly as they said the following words, "Bryan and Penny, we love you. There is nothing that can take that love away. But we also know that it must hurt you horribly to see our children, and we want you to know that if you need to avoid us, it is okay. We love you!"

I was shocked, almost offended with the thought that we would avoid them. That was crazy. They were our dear friends! I responded with a well-meant, but misplaced bravado something like, "Don't worry, we won't do that. It's okay. We love seeing you."

They looked carefully at us, accepted my response, and simply reminded us that they loved us. There was no need to argue. Soon enough the conversation ended and they left to go get their little one. We led them out of the house and I wondered why they felt the need to share what they had said.

As the weeks rolled on and our empty lives marched forward into the cold winter, I noticed that each time we saw their family it cut me to the quick, nearly taking my breath away, like the roaring Wisconsin wind. My mind would automatically compare their precious living children with our dead ones. What would they be doing if they were still alive? How old would they be? Would Caleb run like that? Would Abigail be saying those words now? The questions and comparisons would stir up a blizzard of emotions pelting me, pushing me back, and eventually making me snowbound in my pain.

Ed and Joy were right. They had loved us enough to be brutally honest and give us the freedom to stay away. After a few blizzards, we remembered their permission to avoid them. Now their words no longer offended us. We were relieved. Their deep, healthy love gave us strength to go forward without the added questions of what they might think as we no longer spent time with them. They were true friends for that horrendous season.

In the grand scheme of things they did not know the future, of course, but they acted by principle. And as we would all learn later, their love hinted towards a better time when we would be reunited in ways that none of us could have ever imagined. Even though stars seem relegated to the night, they are in fact, the heralds of the day. Like advance runners, they announce the coming of dawn. They remind us that even when we cannot see the blazing beams of our own star we call the sun, still darkness does not overcome light. So stars remain, and their light is for those who would see the coming of the new day.

Part Three

Dawn

In order for the light
to shine so brightly,
the darkness must be present.

Francis Bacon

Sunrise

The reality is that you will grieve forever.
You will not "get over" the loss of a loved one;
you will learn to live with it.
You will heal and you will rebuild yourself
around the loss you have suffered.
You will be whole again
but you will never be the same.
Nor should you be the same,
nor would you want to.

Elisabeth Kübler-Ross

    I can still remember that morning as I looked into Penny's eyes. I don't actually recall how long it was after the accident, but I am sure it was many months afterwards, and probably more than a year later. We were eating breakfast, becoming very used to eating alone now, and Penny was beginning to cook again. I think we were having some nice toast with jelly on top of it. As I lifted the toast to my mouth, something happened, literally, like the dawn of a new day quietly peeking over the horizon. Penny said the words that moved us out of the dark and into the light.

"Only two people died that day."

We looked at each other. It was true. Her statement was not a question of numeric accuracy, that was obvious. It meant much more.

The accident had been of sufficient enough force to kill all four of us. In 1994, with no airbags in our used car, a rollover accident at sixty miles an hour certainly should have wiped us all out. Yet, I had not even been hurt, and Penny had defied death and brain damage, enabling her to struggle on and live.

Why? That little word which had tormented us for months now invited us to ask, why were we alive? What, or Who, had intervened? Could it be possible that we had a purpose for living? As we stared at each other and the weight of the words settled on us, we began to move towards the illusive place called acceptance.

In the following days, we continued reflecting and searching for answers. We looked back over the previous months, reflecting on the darkness, the pain, the loss of memories. Before the reality of those words Penny had just spoken broke through we would often feel guilty when any kind of laughter occurred. We had no long-term plans. Our dreams were still hijacked regularly by the death of our children, whether in the day or the night. We had not actually begun to live yet. We were effectively existing as shells of who we were before.

Penny's statement pushed us forward.

We did not die, therefore, it must be okay for us to live. For some reason we had been kept alive, and we needed to actually start living again. We suddenly realized it was okay to laugh, dream and hope without being waylaid by feelings of guilt or betrayal. It felt like we were waking up slowly, and rubbing our blurry eyes, we began to realize we had been saved for a purpose.

We were meant to have a future.

As we continued looking back over the dark months that had passed, we connected the dots of the intermittent lights of love from our friends, unexplainable "luck," and saw a beautiful pattern that could not be ignored. Things that some would call happenstance began to multiply until we realized that they were not at all random, but carefully coordinated somehow. Memories revived. We began to see an orchestrated handiwork of something or someone which defied coincidence. Slowly but surely an image of a God working above the chaos began to rise from the ashes, preparing to soar, emblazoned with glory.

We had already known about God, and had had a personal relationship with Him. But when our children died after I had just preached a sermon about faith, and then prayed for protection before traveling home, it radically challenged our perception of God! Amidst our storm of anger and denial, God joined the other casualties of that fatal mishap. Our image of divinity was destroyed. What kind of God could allow such a horrendous thing like this to happen?

I could still feel the echoes from my heart screaming at God, and the questions reverberating in the deepest parts of my mind. How could God be good and allow what had happened? I did not have any easy answer. There is no easy answer. Yet, something nagged at me to consider it again. Amidst my questioning, I was beginning to see that there must be a bigger picture.

Everyone has some sort of a picture of God. Depending on our upbringing, it may be a mono-, poly-, or a-theistic view. In some sense, the polytheistic religions have an easier time explaining the presence of evil and pain, while the atheist doesn't even need to. The great monotheistic, Abrahamic faiths of Judaism, Christianity and Islam, along with a few other smaller faiths, do not have the benefit of assigning the "evil" things in life to another deity or chalking everything up to chance. These monotheistic religions are forced to wrestle for a coherent answer for the darkness.

On a personal level, we each have perceptions of God, and we live our lives either in response to, or rebellion against those pictures. In my life, I had made a serious mistake about my picture of God. For whatever reason, somehow I got it wrong. If the accident had not happened I might never have known it was wrong, because it was all that I knew. But, although I was absolutely sincere, my perception of God was warped, and it took the death of my children to bring it into the light.

I had made the mistake of thinking my relationship with God was built upon what I *did* for Him. I studied and memorized my Bible; I prayed and had devotions; I preached and witnessed; I *did* all the right things and avoided the wrong ones. Notice a pattern? My religion in so many ways was based on what I *did*. As long as I was doing more than others I felt relatively confident and loved. Judgment and comparison were the pillars of my faith. My value before God (and with people, too) was based on my performance and before the accident I thought I was doing pretty well.

Then my children died right before my eyes.

In the early months that followed the accident, as I weathered the storm of grief, all of the things I used to do did not work anymore. In my anger, at times I yelled at God, unable to have any devotional life. While in the middle of depression I didn't want to read anything, cheery or otherwise! I just wanted to die.

One time I honestly tried to jumpstart my faith again by reading a neat book my friend, Dwight Nelson, wrote, called *A New Way to Pray*. In it, he leads the reader into using the words from the Bible to pray, and to let the words of God touch your life. It's a great idea, and truly a blessing for people. But when I tried to do it, I got horribly derailed by the language of the Bible. For example I misheard when the word "terrible" was used. As I read about a Bible figure talking about the "terrible" things God had done ("terrible" meaning "great" and "mighty,") I went crazy with rage! I screamed at God, "yeah God! You have done some pretty terrible things to me, too! Letting my children die in front of me, and now my wife is handicapped, learning how to barely survive! Oh, yeah, terrible things! Thanks a lot, God!!! Go and destroy someone else's life!" That may not seem like much of a rage to you in this world of four-letter words and vulgar expletives, but I have never been a person to swear. Withering sarcasm, metaphorically biting into the flesh of my opponent is my weapon of choice. Yes, I was livid. I threw the Bible away from me and failed to have any meaningful communication with or about God again for months.

I was no longer preaching or even bothering to reach out to others. There was nothing winsome about any part of my life at that point. I was just a man suffering from alternating anger or depression in a tag team performance of abuse.

Penny and I argued a lot. Even though we were intentionally investing in our marriage in an all out war against the specter of divorce, it often seemed that the war was more between us than outside of us. I felt she needed my help to grieve. I needed hers as well. Yet, we both grieved differently, and in an effort to give the other what we needed it caused arguments. Many times in our anger and frustration we would find ourselves wounded and sitting in opposite corners of the house reeling from the words that had been launched at each other. In addition to the pain from words spoken in impatience and anger, we were tormented by the ironic loneliness that comes from hurting and being hurt by the one person who knew and loved us the most.

Trying to be a person of faith and find meaning in the pain, I wanted to pray. I needed help. But if I tried to close my eyes and pray, I would be overwhelmed with another flashback. The pain, fear, and failure would all assault me and send me into a corner shaking uncontrollably. I stopped praying. I know that if anyone had had those same flashbacks, they, too, would have stopped praying also. I decided that I had lost my faith.

Sometime later I shared my belief that I had lost my faith with our counselor and simply said, "Frank, I think I am no longer a believer because I can't do all the things I used to do." He listened and asked me to explain why I felt that way. I told him that I couldn't do anything anymore with—or for—God. All the things I used to do were impotent, and my anger at my loss was pointed directly to heaven. How could God allow my precious children to die? Then he said something I will never forget.

Intently looking into my eyes, he paused and spoke these words into my life, "Bryan, it is not what you do for God that builds your relationship; it is what God does for you! Right now you are broken and there is nothing you can do. Let God hold you and *love you* in your brokenness!" He went on to relate how our great God, the Creator of all humanity, has been passionately pursuing us in every part of life. We don't choose Him. He has already chosen us! Amazing. Anyone who has been a part of a faith community has probably heard those words many times before, but it seems as if we simply take a part of them and add them to our faulty picture of God, just like I did. I still equated my value with who I was instead of who God is. What a colossal difference!

Maybe you could call a portion of my story, *Confessions of a Legalist*, because God literally had to break me in order to get me to see it. But that afternoon as Frank helped me to see God's amazing love in the midst of my being unable to do *anything*, it changed me. Light started to shine through.

I began to see the God of Abraham as a God of deep, abiding, passionate love, who was pursuing me and orchestrating events to set me free. One verse in particular took on new meaning to me. In Jeremiah 31:3, God says to the people after a horrendous time of judgment and brokenness, "Yes, I have loved you with an everlasting love; Therefore with lovingkindness I have drawn you."

Imagine that. I had the impression that I needed to bring God to others, or confront them with some theological belief before they could be loved and saved. But no, on that day I began to realize that God is the

One moving and acting first. We don't choose Him, He chooses us! Like a tractor beam from Star Trek, the great God of the universe is literally drawing us to Himself. Amazing thought.

After meeting with Frank, I shared this new revelation to Penny. We weighed what it meant. We began to see a different framework on how to view God. Could it actually be true?

I like to share the contrast of what we saw that day this way. Imagine a young child running to see his father who was already fully aware of his child's whereabouts and was intently watching. In the process, the child falls on the unforgiving asphalt and horribly scrapes and cuts his knees, hands, and head. There is blood, deep cuts, and pain. Cries erupt. The father quickly runs to his side and gently picks him up, holding and caring for the wounds but more importantly, his child. There are words of comfort and encouragement, not of judgment. Time stands still as love enfolds the hurting child.

Most of us can imagine such a picture, because we know most of the time parents genuinely want the very best for their offspring. Yet, in my actions, I had a warped view of God. I did not see that side. I seemed to have had another picture for some reason.

Imagine another father simply standing afar off, judging the child's performance as the young boy pushes himself to earn approval, and goes faster and farther. Then the immature feet hit a rise in the road, and the runner comes crashing down. As the boy cries out in pain, the father remains where he is, yells to his son to get up again, and keep running; telling him to try not to fall again and go faster; keep running!

What a cold contrast. Frank had invited us to see God more like the first father, not the second! But my picture of Him had actually been more like the second. Now, in our horrendous brokenness, Penny and I could not run. We had nothing to give, nothing more to prove. We were broken. Could it be that God was holding us in our pain, giving us the time to heal? The words came back over and over, "Let God love you!" Sure, eventually (maybe), there would be time to run again, but it would not be for a long time. Even the very reason for running would also change. We no longer had to prove our worth to anyone because of that amazing love.

This new component of God's grace and love poured into our broken hearts and began to bring healing. It was not immediate, and took months to mature. We were learning to let God love us. We no longer thought we had to perform in order to find acceptance. We were loved just as we were, even in our brokenness. It was okay to just hurt, and let love hold us. As we chose to believe those words we began to look for other messages of unmerited love and acceptance.

Once again we opened our aching hearts to the encouraging words of the Bible. The stories of faith and miracles performed pulled us towards hope. The forgiveness and patience revealed in God's interaction throughout history invited us to see a longer exposure of grace and mercy than we had first imagined. A new picture of God was developing.

In the warm embrace of love, the infected boils of pain crusted over and began to dry up. As we received love from God we were more patient with each other. The explosive anger dissolved. As the depression slowly lifted, we could gradually see farther ahead than we had for months. So, because we had been letting God love us, we found ourselves at breakfast that morning staring face to face and making the monumental realization that only two people died in the accident that day. That statement triggered a paradigm shift in our world. What did it mean?

Could it be that the loving God had spared us for something more? Could it be that He wanted us to experience His divine Love in ways which we never even knew we needed? Is it possible that in the grand scheme of things Caleb and Abigail had lost nothing except pain and sickness? Is it possible that when they are raised from the dead (as is taught by all the books of the Abrahamic religions), that they will grow up in a place where love reigns rather than sin? If these things might be true, then what did this amazing God of love have in mind for Penny and me now?

As we pondered those questions, little ideas began to sprout like seeds of hope in the broken furrows of our hearts, watered by all the tears of the months before. They now began the process of growing into a harvest of hope. The winter was passing, and spring was dawning.

The sun truly was beginning to rise with healing in its wings, inviting us to the next days of our lives.

Worship

Worship is the submission
of all of our nature to God.
It is the quickening of conscience by His holiness,
nourishment of mind by His truth,
purifying of imagination by His beauty,
opening of the heart to His love,
and submission of will to His purpose.
And all of this gathered up in adoration
is the greatest of human expressions
of which we are capable.

William Temple

Have you ever gone outside on an early spring morning to just sit, listening in the dark, right before dawn? The crisp air tugs at your exposed skin reminding you to pull your coat down a little lower. Your eyes roam about, waiting for the moment when light will pierce the darkness. Finally, as the sun majestically strides up over the horizon with colors colliding in the first rush hour of the day, you simply have to marvel in rapt attention to this daily phenomena of nature. As the colors emerge and you find yourself marveling at the beauty, you begin to realize you are not alone. If you are in the woods, you will hear the rustling of the birds and their morning melodies announcing their presence and praise for a new day.

Many religions have seen the dawn as an important part of our worship, or the first moment when we can turn our hearts to the God who has given us life again after a night of sleep. It's not that we worship the object of creation, as some religions certainly do, but instead use the time to focus on what is most important. Like the birds waking up and singing their songs in the morning, we have the choice to turn our hearts towards God and begin the day in worship.

Though this seems very normal in the routine of life, the reality is that the sun rises each day, and many of us never truly experience what that means! For days on end we may oversleep this seminal moment and simply go on ignoring or taking for granted the mighty miracle of each new day. But at times, interspersed and interrupting the routine, distinct moments come when the scientific fact of a new day becomes a metaphysical reality. The realization of the day moves us into a new chapter of our lives.

This is a time when we can begin to see the world around us in new light, and time moves forward. We step into a world of worship and wonder. I believe we have each experienced, at one time or another, these moments when life becomes very focused and you know that something new is approaching on the horizon. A new light shines when you realize there is more to life than just you, and that there is still hope—for you—for a better future.

After our "sunrise" moment, Penny and I began to see our lives differently than before. We both were attending school, now that Penny had recuperated as much as she ever would, and we settled down into student life. We enjoyed driving together to the University of Wisconsin-Whitewater each day and immersing ourselves in study. Arriving on campus, Penny and I went off to very different buildings. She had chosen to continue her social work degree because of her love for people in general, and children specifically. I was relegated to more math classes than most people care or even dare to think of (outside of other science and engineering nuts like me)!

Reconnecting over lunch was a daily delight as we effectively began to date each other again in this new chapter of our lives. We had been warned that we would need to intentionally fight for our marriage in order to stay together after such a tragedy. Statistically, we had an 85% divorce rate stalking us! So, in the face of that threat, we took it as a challenge to grow in our love and communication skills. We learned to intentionally take time to listen to each other and truly ask questions, trying to hear each others' hearts. On a large university campus there were many other choices and people who could have caught our eyes or our interest. Therefore we did not take each other and our choice of each other for granted. We invested in each other and our future together. After a full day of classes or study, we cherished the drive home talking about our day. Ironically, our daily time in the car became a sacred, life-giving space.

We also had great opportunities to build more shared, new memories by going to concerts and plays. Learning to be young adults without children was quite a change and we gave ourselves permission to even let it be fun! We noticed our freedom even more in this season of change when we realized it was time for both of us to begin living again. Musical programs from around the world, with different cultures displaying the themes of life in different ways enlarged and enriched us. They invited us to dream of new adventures together. The moving drama performances provided a soothing salve to our wounds. The comedy routines caused us to squint at life differently with our stomach muscles aching. Month after month, almost imperceptibly, the arts plied away the deadness of our aching hearts. Laughter and love began walking more regularly with us again.

We made new friends and started to socialize again. It was good to open up with others and begin to make fresh memories. But we noticed something. Life, like the arts, coalesces both pain and joy. While the noise of life and the commotion of activity filled our days, we knew that most people would walk by us and never know that our hearts were gaping holes of pain and loss. Sure, we still functioned and lived. But we were just shells of who we could be. But we made an important discovery. We realized that many others were also slinking shadows. We could see it in their eyes when they thought no one was looking. We could hear it when a slight crack in their voices betrayed their deep aching. We began to notice the telltale signs. Because of our experience with such deep pain, we could sense their hurt. The symphony of pain unites musicians from every walk of life, and the conductor of loss marks each one. So our lives moved on, walking and stumbling, getting back up with a little more awareness of others around us who were hurting too. As we learned to let God hold us day by day, we started noticing the chords of compassion rising above the deep bass notes of pain. We could see the same God who was holding us was also touching and working in our friends' lives at their deepest points of need. Our new relationships were filled with rich times of wounded worship as we walked together through this painful journey called life.

Church began to change as well. It would be more appropriate to say that our response to church changed. We went for different reasons than before. We did not go because we "had to," and no longer felt guilty if we did not attend. There were times when we simply could not play the "smiling game" and we would stay home to worship or feel overcome by our hurt there alone. If we went, it was because we wanted to worship God and love people. Otherwise, we stayed away and would not hypocritically show up.

Somewhere in the course of our experiencing grief we were deeply encouraged by a sign that was apparently hanging in one psychologist's room. I don't remember if there was any special border or color scheme which played about it, but the words are forever etched in my mind. They have set us free from a thousand different religious tormentors: "Today, I will not SHOULD on myself!" What an amazing and bold statement of healthy boundaries.

Because of that sign, and the truth it enshrines, we started practicing the habit of not "should"-ing on ourselves. [Just a note here: please correctly enunciate that word carefully if reading this out loud or sharing the idea in churches like I have many times—it has a tendency to wake up people who have poor hearing!] Any time either of us noticed hearing the word "should" repeatedly taking center stage in a sentence or our thinking, it would raise a red flag.

If one of us caught the other saying things like, "I think we *should* go and visit so and so;" or "I really *should* eat less of that;" or, "I *should* not think or feel that way;" etc., we would speak up and ask, "Okay fine, but do you *want* to do that?" We would stop ourselves and ask what we actually would choose to do, not what we felt compelled to do.

In this stage of our healing we were learning to be intentional with our choices. We were no longer victims to circumstances, we were learning that we had a choice in our reactions and decisions. The words from our sunrise moment echoed over and over in our minds: only two people died on December 3, 1994, and for some reason, God had given us a choice to live! Our path to emotional health required setting healthy boundaries and limits. We learned to say "no" or "yes" without guilt as we endeavored to be true to ourselves and our choices. We began to stop *shoulding* on ourselves.

As I try to understand grief and share with others the metaphors I see, this time of dawn and worship puzzles me. Whether it relates to grief or other challenges in life, does the act of worship, or acceptance of the night, bring the dawn and usher us out of the dark; or, does the inevitable timing of the event create the worship? In other words, what made us move into the light? Was it the passing of time only? Remember, the sun rises each day. So what makes some dawns more liminal than others? Was it the decision to accept that we were still alive that made that day count?

Or, is there a third option? Could it be that God, Himself, decides when darkness has done enough of its work and He allows the gentle bursting of the sun to announce the presence of a new day and a new time, with the result that that gift naturally calls forth the worship of the soul?

I'm not sure I know the complete answer. I know our choices don't speed up time (it is beyond our control), and if a person does not appropriately give grief its time they can become locked in denial; but, I also know that time alone does not heal our pain and move us to acceptance. There seems to be a curious relationship between worship and choice that is worth pondering.

Worship and choice seem to be bound together. Worship, the surrendering of our lives to God, cannot exist without choice. Choice implies there is something or someone bigger than us allowing us to even make that choice. Revelation invites worship. Then, worship pushes us to more choices, thereby leading to more worship, and on, and on, in a limitless cycle.

Let me illustrate this a little more.

One morning while we were relaxing at home in our living room, each of us were having some personal worship time. At that time something burst into my world that I cannot even begin to comprehend. Without any fanfare Penny picked her head up from what she was reading and looked at me. Her face displayed the fact that she was about to say something very important, so I paused from what I was doing and acknowledged her.

Then her lips began to move and she said the following words, "we really should pray for Susan Smith."

For those of you who may not recognize that name anymore, Susan Smith deliberately chose to kill her young children. According to the story, she strapped her children into their car seats, leaving them in the vehicle, pushed the vehicle into the lake, and stood guard until the stream of air bubbles escaping the sinking tomb finally slowed to a stop. She waited until the car was fully submerged and then went to a pay phone and reported that her car had been stolen. A huge search ensued for a few days until the truth finally shook clear and her deception rose to life, unlike her missing children who were dead at the bottom of the lake. In the wake of the horrendous story that came to light, she was eventually tried and put into prison.

So, Penny said again, "we really should pray for Susan Smith."

My wife had just said we should pray for her? Was this a "should" should? Or, did she actually mean she wanted to pray for her?

I am not proud of the first thoughts that immediately filled my head, but they were most certainly angry. My first thought was: pray for her? Are you crazy? What would you like us to pray for? Do you want to pray that she rots in hell for the horrendous thing that she did as a mother, murdering her own babies? What do you mean? Just what exactly are we supposed to pray for? The thoughts in my mind exploded with confusion and rage.

My face must have betrayed my baffled brain, so Penny paused longer allowing my mind to grapple with this apparently colossal contradiction. Here before me was a mother who had lost her own two children, now stone cold dead in Michigan. Yet, for some reason, my broken, hurting wife wanted to pray for a woman who, in a pre-meditated act of deception and treachery, killed her own children? How on earth, and why, could my wife be wanting to pray for her?

Penny looked at me and then she said the words that changed me. Calmly and gently, as though she was realizing the impact that these words were about to have on my whole worldview, she said, "she must have been hurting very badly to have ever thought that her actions were helping her children."

What?

Where did that come from? What was she talking about?

My amazing wife had just literally stepped outside of her world of pain and, with compassion, was able to look upon someone like Susan Smith and see her best possible heart. Unlike all of the normal human reactions of revenge, retribution and hatred, my wife was speaking for the heart of the Divine One who sees our greatest needs and our broken desires and longs to set us free, the One who can look behind the desperate actions and painful responses and see, instead, a heart that is itself desperately longing for love.

There in that morning time of worship, from her own broken and decimated heart, God had so filled my wife with love that she was able to love another person like that. I was dumbfounded.

I felt like falling on my knees before God and crying out. Here before me was a woman robbed of her own children, yet because of the love given to her in her darkest and deepest chasms of pain, she was then willing to choose to extend love and compassion to another! Like that moment when Corrie Ten Boom met the Nazi guard who was complicit in the death of her sister and countless others asking her to forgive him; and her arm seemed frozen until the onslaught of grace thawed both heart and hand, allowing her to shake his hand in forgiveness. Or, the untold times when Mother Teresa would bend over the mangled mess of humanity before her, literally pouring her life out in service with no chance of repayment or need for praise. What allows someone to love and respond like that?

Before my very eyes I was witnessing another burning bush. The amazing, passionate heart throb of God bursting from within the shell of my precious and broken Penny. It was my personal collision with grace, where I saw the unmistakable, self-sacrificing character of God's love standing in the face of my dark and depraved self. Convicted to my very core, I surrendered and chose to let that passionate love transform me, too.

That's worship!

Blessings

*It is doubtful whether
God can bless a man greatly
until He has hurt him deeply.*

A. W. Tozer

You might be wondering why I chose to study mathematics given that I seem to be involved more in a life of ministry now. It's a fair question since math might seem to be a strange choice. I chose math because I did not want to add any more stress to our lives after the children died. Although I would have preferred it, searching for a school which offered a religious degree would have involved moving away to another area. So, we chose to remain near our home, and I simply chose something I enjoyed doing. I also assumed it would be a degree involving few emotions, and I thought I could probably do it without too much trauma. I was correct as far as the emotions were concerned, but the mental strain was quite involved. In fact, one of my professors remarked one day how math was such a very safe world to run into! I'm not sure his statement was a very healthy one, however!

Our time at the university was peaceful and a time of healing for us as we settled into the next chapter of our lives. Penny became more and more used to using only one hand, and most of her other pains went away, apart from the ever-present phantom nerve pain in her left arm. We were grateful to be alive.

As I neared the completion of my degree to be a high school mathematics teacher, we made the decision to apply to go back overseas to Micronesia, knowing that there were always great needs there. The organization we applied to responded quickly, and we were given the opportunity to go to the island of Yap. They needed a principal for a K-12 school there.

I had only just finished my teaching degree, and here were people asking if I would be a principal of a full, K-12 school system! I guess interesting things can happen when an organization has a need and you are simply willing. It's more like this: they were desperate and I was willing! It was a good combination.

So, one month after finishing my degree in 1997, Penny and I prepared to move. We packed, stored, sold, or gave away all of our stuff, then wept as we said our goodbyes to friends who were, in many ways, closer than family. Hand-in-hand, we traveled back to the land where we had met years before. Since Yap is a different state in the country of Micronesia, in a sense, it was a new beginning for us.

Moving to a new place always has its unique challenges and unknowns. One day we were in the USA, unmoved by the banality of our known world, and within twenty hours the airplane door opened and our senses were immersed into a land of swaying coconut trees, succulently fresh pineapple, ubiquitous betel nut stains, and salty ocean breezes. What a transition of time and space. As we slipped down the steps and waded through the undulating heat waves towards the simple airport building, each step made impressions on the asphalt due to the unrelenting heat and sunshine. Little did we know how much this land would also leave its mark on us in the months ahead.

Arriving on the campus an hour later where our humble two-bedroom apartment would be both our place of work and home, we settled into our new surroundings. With Penny's healthy disdain for any and all bugs, she immediately went to war making the apartment clean enough for her standards. I worked at unpacking our things and surveying the campus and facilities of my new world. Hours later, the sweat of the tropics welcomed us to our first night as we lay there exhausted, yet excited in our new home. We liked our new beginning.

Within days the honeymoon period was over as the various roles of trying to lead a full school system exploded before me. The change was numbing, even horrifying. I had literally just finished being a number in a university system with 12,000 students, and now I was the principal of the most respected school on an island of 12,000 people! With one plane flight I had traversed the distance from student to teacher to leader! It took me awhile to realize the full impact of that change, but ready or not, the year was coming.

We had one month before classes would begin, and that meant there were repairs to be made, uniforms to be arranged, parents to visit, and a trip to Hawaii to pick up new teachers. Because our school ran on the backs of yearly volunteers coming from various colleges (like Penny and I had previously done), there was no consistency apart from the principal. That meant we were in for some serious learning curves. Added to that was the fact that the school was more than $100,000 in debt. It became pretty clear why the organization had been desperate enough to hire me!

From our perspective, however, it was a great way to learn a new work, since basically we figured it could only improve from where it was. The first bright, ray of hope came when we were teamed with an older, more experienced accountant, JoAnn, and her husband, Bill, the maintenance director, who helped give us stability in our adventure. We discovered we made a great team, and things started to go very well. We were so grateful for their help. They were both so patient with us as we learned. The year took off without too many hitches, and life began to settle in.

One day after church about three months into our stay, one of the church members came up and asked us a question. Since people had heard our story and tried to understand the pain we had experienced losing Caleb and Abigail, it was not unusual for people to come up and offer care and support. The pain was still quite raw and evident in our lives even though we were trying to serve and be a blessing to others. People seemed to appreciate the transparency and the openness in which we lived our lives in the face of the pain.

So, when she came up to talk with us we were not surprised. However what she said caught us completely off-guard.

She asked us, "Would you like to consider adopting an unborn child?"

Would we? Our hearts leapt! Our eyes probably betrayed the deep longing to love again after being decimated with the loss of our first two children. We didn't think we would ever have children of our own again because Penny always had had difficult pregnancies, and I had had a difficult reversal after the accident (which did not come with any guarantees for accuracy or potency!) So even though we wanted to love again, all we could do was simply pray, do our part, and hope. Her question immediately captured our interest, so we told her we would be happy to meet with the birth mother.

The next day, we went to see a young woman who was willing to do something out of the ordinary within her culture, something requiring exceptional bravery. Adoptions are not unusual for other island cultures necessarily, but for this particular island it was considered to be unacceptable and very rare—even offensive. Because of some family situations and her commitment to the life of her child, she was unwilling to abort her baby and had gone to her relative to ask if they would take care of her baby after birth. Having a relative raise your child was a fairly common practice. Because the island was less than thirty square miles in size, the reality was that birth mothers would, in all likelihood, see their children again! This young woman's relative responded that they were unable to help, and were, in fact, even struggling to provide for their own children. But the relative did say that they knew of a young couple who might have an interest in adopting her baby. Such was the beginning of events stranger than fiction, which would be nearly unbelievable to me had I not lived them!

Following the directions of the church member, we wound our way to her home, anxiously wondering what we might find. Finally, we arrived. We sat with very little small talk, meeting with this woman, hearing her story, and observing the home she lived in. We watched her chew betel nut, then spit its red, foul-smelling juices out through the floor slats of her porch. She assured us she had stopped drinking alcohol as soon as she found out she was pregnant. In addition to our questions, she asked us a few questions about our story and our expectations for the future. It was a surreal moment. There she was, offering to give us her precious child in an act of ultimate motherly care, while we wrestled with a desperate longing to have a child again. Neither party could be objective in that situation. It was an obviously orchestrated event set up by the amazing God of love.

After our short interview together, we told this young mother that we would pray about it before giving her our final answer, though in our minds we sensed it would not take long.

Looking back, I'm amazed, realizing what God was actually doing. You may remember that when Penny and I began our relationship, I was reluctant to have children. My reluctance had caused regular tension, difficulty, and dysfunction in our marriage while Caleb and Abigail were alive. After their death, of course, I carried tremendous guilt and remorse. Then, after a time of healing and the rekindling of our love for each other, we were being given a choice: do we want to have children again?

It was literally a gift and an invitation from God asking us, more specifically *me*, if I was ready yet. Would I choose to let Him bless us? The beautiful change was that now, in the wake of what we had experienced, in my brokenness and in His incredible love throughout the darkness, we were ready. I was ready to choose to be a father again. It seems that many times our choices can either open or shut a door to God's blessings.

So, within a few days we contacted the young mother, visited her again, and agreed that we would be willing to adopt her child. We didn't know if the baby would be healthy, or if there would be any lingering effects from her lifestyle choices. We had no idea what to expect. Due to some other extenuating circumstances, we were unable to meet the father. From that point on we took her to all her maternal care appointments. My wife would sit and listen as the doctor found the heartbeat, checked blood pressure and measured the growing baby bump to make sure all was well. We waited until finally we received the important phone call we had been waiting for.

About one o'clock in the morning on Thanksgiving day, the phone rang and the young mother told us that we should come and pick her up and take her to the hospital. We felt unmanageable joy as we drove to her house, bouncing and rattling through the potholes in the asphalt road until we turned off that "nice" road to go onto what can only could be described as an island, off-road path. We picked her up in the school's pickup truck which only had space for two in the front. So my wife bravely got into the back of the pickup truck, preparing to hang on and be bounced all around. Heading towards the hospital, I drove more slowly, hoping the baby would not be born in the pickup truck before our arrival! For the next several hours I waited in the hallway while Penny witnessed an incredible double miracle. She witnessed the miracle of a precious life being born, but also one of God giving us a child again.

A healthy baby boy! As his hearty screams reverberated through the room, our hearts joined his in rejoicing at the thought of being able to love again. Energy and praise flowed between us as we held his warm skin for the first time on that never-to-be-forgotten Thanksgiving Day! The hours in the hospital were spent holding him close and caring for him, watching the rats scurry from room to room. We humorously noted how the nurses completely changed their response to his needs when they realized he was being adopted by the American couple. From the beginning when we made our decision to adopt her baby, his birth mother changed the way she would talk about him. From that point on she always called him, "our baby." She was, in a sense, distancing herself from him so she could go forward with this incredibly difficult decision. It was a very motherly and compassionate act for her to be willing to give her child to us, and we are eternally grateful. She had also stipulated we could name him whatever we wanted because he was our boy. We deeply contemplated what would be a name worthy of such a gift.

As we prayed and pondered, something deep welled up from within us. We wanted a name encompassing some of our greatest dreams for this little gift from God. Someone bold, strong, standing for righteousness and truth, who didn't have to die. Penny and I hate death, and we wanted this child to have a name that could almost invoke an immunity to that invading force against life. Our minds went back to the story of the prophet, Elijah, whose very name means "Jehovah/Yahweh is my God." Elijah was one who stood true to principle and even defied death in a blazing chariot ride to heaven! As we held our Elijah, we spoke his name with a prayer that he would grow mighty in God, knowing who He was, and stand for right regardless of what the world did around him. Finally, with whatever the future held for all of us, we hoped he would also one day cheat death by living faithfully in God's strength until the return of Jesus Christ.

Rejoicing in the light of the next day, we paid the total hospital bill of $30 for both mommy and baby. And, with Elijah in our arms, we left the hospital.

Our big, brown bundle of blessing was coming home!

Laughter

Laughter
is the closest thing
to the grace of God.

Karl Barth

The first days at home with our precious Elijah evoked a vast array of emotions and experiences. Tears of joy flowed freely as we looked into his perfectly cute face. We loved squeezing his slightly rounded cheeks. Parental memories came back in the dark of night with the various techniques needed to hold and care for a little hungry one again. I could even rejoice in diapers while the first few times remembering to do the quick dodge and cover moves necessary for little boys! Often we were momentarily mesmerized while staring at this beautiful bundle of God's goodness to us, hoping against hope that it could actually be true.

There were many unknowns ahead of us. International adoptions are by no means easy or free, and we had been warned that the process was daunting. The first few days we cautiously answered the phone or eyed everyone new coming by the school, fearful his birth mother, father, or another relative might change their minds and come to take him away from us.

How was it all going to work out? We didn't know but we were too filled with love and joy again to see very far ahead. Almost blindly we went forward with the process, trusting in God's goodness and overwhelmed with awe each time we saw Elijah resting in his bed. His gentle breathing brought back the bittersweet memories of our other children, yet whispered hope in the face of the unknown.

There are usually two processes complicating overseas adoptions. The first is the legal aspect of the child becoming yours which requires working with both governments. The second is satisfying the immigration issues allowing you to leave one country and then enter your own. Being forewarned, we chose to go forward, regardless. What unfolded before us amazed us. God's blessings and fingerprints were all over the entire process.

First of all, because we were in Micronesia, the laws were patterned after United States laws and, therefore, fell under the same adoption "non-sticky" requirements. What was required by Micronesia was sufficient for the United States. Second, Micronesian citizens were able to enter the USA freely, without any special immigration needs due to a unique relationship between the two governments; there were no special fees associated, or needed. Thirdly, because we were living in Yap and serving as volunteers, we qualified to have a regional law agency prepare our papers on a sliding scale. That meant with our low income, compared to Guam standards, our adoption papers were filed and the court procedure all processed *free of charge*!

We could not believe it. Within months of our arrival in this new place, God was in the process of miraculously giving us an internationally adopted baby boy for a mind boggling sum of $30! Unheard of! But God was not finished with His blessings.

In the midst of all the preparations for Elijah's birth, and the busy day-to-day requirements of running a school, life had been very full. We had so many changes to manage and deal with that another part of our lives seemed to be forgotten. With the diminished odds from the previous operation I had chosen to have and the known challenges of Penny's pregnancies, we had effectively given up our dream of having another child naturally.

Until Penny noticed she was not feeling well. At first we figured she was just exhausted and sleep-deprived, caring for our newborn. But then the symptoms just did not make sense. Afraid to hope, waiting a few more days, thinking it may have been some bad food or some kind of virus, we tried to put it out of our minds. But, hope is a persistent flower and when God gives it life it cannot be kept down, piercing even a blanket of frozen, dead leaves.

Finally, the night before the court proceedings to make Elijah completely ours, Penny could wait no longer. She decided to take a pregnancy test. Frozen with anticipation, I waited, trying to contain a squirming Elijah in my arms, listening for any signs of a result. Could it be? Or, would it be just another false hope, dashed like many before? Moments later, Penny emerged with a look of utter shock, and holding in her one good hand a white dipstick with two red lines, boldly announcing a positive result!

She was pregnant!

Waves of tears, shouts of praise, and moments of mute amazement overwhelmed us. We could not believe it. With one newborn in our arms, we were now being invited to consider that we were going to have another baby! God was too good to us!

That night passed quickly with little sleep between feeding Elijah and crying out with joy at the miracles surrounding us. Early the next morning we dressed him and prepared to go to the court for the final determination of Elijah's adoption. The process had gone by much faster than anyone had anticipated. He was almost officially ours.

The event itself was quite unremarkable, and I don't even remember what the judge looked like. All the paperwork had been professionally prepared and provided, and the birth mother had signed away her rights, thereby allowing us to adopt our little Elijah. There had been no hitches. It seemed literally, "too good to be true!" The judge simply asked us what our plans were to provide for him, and as we answered briefly about our situation and desire to bless and love Elijah like our own, he was satisfied. Speaking his agreement as he signed the papers in front of him, the judge directed us to go and wait for the official documents to be released from another room. Moments later, we held Elijah's birth certificate listing us as his parents, and all the necessary adoption documents proving he was legally ours.

We stood motionless, silent, as though we were on holy ground.

Looking more closely at the paperwork, eyeing the details of each line and signature in our hands, it seemed the ground around us began to tremble. There, before us with the official seal of the Micronesian government, was the date of December 3, 1997. The meaning burst upon us! In our rush of preparing everything for Elijah's arrival, we had not realized it, but now it was finally breaking through. *Exactly three years to the day* when our precious Caleb and Abigail died, we were now holding in our hands and in Penny's womb, two more children!

Like scientists recording the warning tremors and active steam vents announcing eminent volcanic activity, we quickly connected the events and realized each individual part of our story pointed to this culmination of God's care. God himself seemed to be exploding with joy and laughter, reveling in His ability to bless! Shell-shocked in that eruption of worship, we joined heaven with tears of gratitude running hot down our faces.

Stunning!

Consider that, three years to the day of our devastation, God gave us children to love again. I stand in awe at His amazing goodness. The God of love who held us in our darkest places, and had drawn us to Himself was now showing another aspect of His character.

Just as we had found solace in the revelation of His true character of love from Jeremiah 31:3, "Yes, I have loved you with an everlasting love; Therefore with lovingkindness I have drawn you," we were now led to learn another principle. This God of love was also the God who had a plan for our lives, and we were learning that it was a good plan! From the same book, just a few pages over in Jeremiah 29:11, we found these words, "For I know the thoughts that I think toward you, says the Lord, thoughts of peace and not of evil, to give you a future and a hope." In some intricate design of heaven, at just the right time, God was fulfilling these words to us. This plan could not take away the excruciating pain we felt from losing Caleb and Abigail, yet somehow God seemed to be inviting us to see a bigger picture of what He was doing. Knowing He was in control brought us to a place of peace and joy.

In the grand questions of faith and life, some may claim coincidence and fail to see the majesty, but at some point the numeric odds begin to be ludicrous. There was no way to have humanly designed the events leading up to this convergence culminating in Elijah's birth. His conception months before, the mother's fear for the future of her child, relinquishing control, pondering various choices, meeting and choosing an unknown couple who had only been on the island three months, and his birth on Thanksgiving Day were all in perfect timing. Then Penny getting pregnant at exactly the same time, and just learning about it; and Elijah's paperwork being finalized as fast as it did, and in the way it happened so inexpensively.

Serendipity?

No way!

Of course, people are free to choose to randomly wander through happenstance with the meaningfulness of all moments dissolving into a matrix of chance, but in the light of what God has shown us, I choose to walk reverently in worshipful wonder of a caring Creator who promises to have a plan for my life that coalesces time and space for good! I certainly cannot explain how God arranges all these things, and why certain things happen that are so horrendous, but the principle remains that there is a plan. Learning to live this way changes all the rules of life. We can learn to trust the goodness of God in the face of the unknown.

Returning to the school with our faces literally glowing with the evidences of God's goodness, and the joy of having Elijah safely ours, we settled into our new life. The school year moved on, and now in addition to raising Elijah, we had to deal with Penny's difficult pregnancy in a foreign place. In yet another evidence of God's providence, the local pastor's wife living near us was a doctor, and she helped provide some timely IV's when Penny needed them. The days quickly ran into each other, bumping the weeks into months and our first year ended quickly.

Immediately after finishing my first successful year as a principal, I loaded my enlarged wife and son onto a plane bound for Guam to await the birth of our second miracle child. After some time spent waiting and enjoying peaceful moments away from responsibilities, we were once again blessed by God with a healthy, beautiful baby girl we named Hannah. From the very beginning she captured our hearts. Our home was four again! Amazed and challenged by God's goodness to us, we quickly realized there are good reasons for separating the births of children by ten or more months! Having Elijah and Hannah less than eight months apart made them biologically impossible to duplicate, and actually more difficult to handle than twins. It seemed God's plan for us did not include boredom! Those two became our ever-present sidekicks, and Penny began to grow and mature as a fantastic re-made mom.

We eventually finished our two year commitment and prepared to return to the USA with our new family.

God had blessed not only our family, but the school as well. Through a number of unforeseen turns and guided decisions, the school was debt-free and growing as we prepared to go forward to whatever God had next for us. In yet another telltale sign of God's guidance, we were hired over the phone by the new principal, sight unseen, to replace a mathematics teacher of twenty-eight years at the very same academy at which we were working when Caleb and Abigail died. We were about to return home to the people who loved us, with our ready-made, God-given family!

Again, however, we don't do normal. In the process of planning to return to the USA, we arranged to bring four, bright, Yapese teenage girls back with us to finish their schooling in Wisconsin. That was crazy! Why on earth would someone choose to have two children under the age of two, and four girls between the ages of seventeen to nineteen? Upon reflection, it seems a bit strange to us as well.

Part of the challenge with experiencing such impressive mountaintops of God's grace is that we have to fight the natural process of moving from the miraculous to the mundane. The human tendency is to forget and slide back down into "normal" again, and forget what it is like up on the mountain. Even though God wants to lead us higher and still higher to more of His goodness, after literally lighting our faces with glory after glory, we often "settle down" too soon, and remain in the valley and comfort of the known. I guess one of the things Penny and I do to avoid this is to not be normal! We want to see more of God's goodness. It's okay if others think that we are crazy! Many times we feel it ourselves, but what an amazing way to live: on God's radical edge!

Our hearts were in the right place. We wanted to be a blessing to the girls. I believe we were. But it was an incredibly challenging year coming back to the USA with our own transitions as a family again, on top of their own collisions with our culture, cold weather, and an American standard school system.

I'm sure heaven laughed again as the eight of us paraded single file through the Guam airport on our journey to the United States. There was much the girls had never seen before. Yap only had one building with three stories, and there were no elevators or escalators. So, as they approached the moving steps of the escalator the leader stopped so suddenly and without warning that the others slammed into her back so hard it nearly sent all of them crashing down like a waterfall of tumbling black hair! After some subdued screaming and coaching we got them separated, and they experienced their first ride down a moving staircase, much to the humor of everyone watching and waiting.

Many hours and various other travel adventures later, we arrived in Wisconsin and all eight of us moved into our new house. The local folks called us the Yap gang and our home was marked by a handmade, concrete rendition of Yapese stone money. There were so many new things for the girls to experience: traffic, snow, large grocery stores and much more in the months to come. For us, so many reminders and moments of healing came as we shared our miracle children with our friends.

In another touch of God's delight, our next door neighbors were none other than our friends from before, Ed and Joy! They had moved in right next door to us, and now we were able to rekindle our friendships and watch our children grow up side-by-side again. Hugging them brought tears of joy, realizing all that God had done in our lives.

What an amazing turn of events within such a short period of time! Looking back on our experience is like shooting the whitewater rapids of life with God's grace, mercy, and strength upholding us above the rocks. Sure, we were often drenched by tears and drained at times in the exhilarating turns and bounces, but in the moments of peace and quiet as we looked back on where we had gone, we realized that a life of trusting God was never dull! Even in the deepest canyons with their walls momentarily eclipsing the sunlight, we could hear the reassuring and steady calls of our Guide rising above the tumult around us, leading us further into the unknown, with His inviting laughter, inspiring us with hope for whatever was to come next!

Part Four

Destiny

*A ship in harbor is safe,
but that is not
what ships are built for.*

John A. Shedd

Empathy

Only people who are capable of loving strongly
can also suffer great sorrow,
but this same necessity of loving
serves to counteract their grief
and heals them.

Leo Tolstoy

The ubiquitous presence of pain and suffering in the world remains one of the most challenging subjects confronting people of faith. How can one claim there is a good and all-powerful God in the face of such unspeakable suffering? Why do bad things happen to good people? Such questions can silence the most devout scholar and empower the boldest atheist. Untold authors, from within or outside of the scriptures, have endeavored to parry off the attack and offer a counter-response, but the wounds remain.

Although I have shared some of the windows into our world and the seeming coherence we have found in the face of pain, I know it is not an easy subject. Certainly, to discount the depth of this problem is to fail to comprehend its significance. Oftentimes we resort to trite answers and short responses, hoping the questions will be forgotten or go away. Yet, they don't, and they won't! I have wrestled with these questions for many years. I still have many questions. Whatever faith I have today is not from the absence of questioning, but from the evidence of goodness in the midst of the doubt. I do not mock this question and I certainly do not blame anyone for doubting. Even in a matrix of hope, which brings an alignment to the purpose and plan for our lives, there remain many unknowns and doubts.

There are certain side effects of going through such a traumatic experience as we did. One of those is the realization of the incredible depths of pain one can be thrust into. There have been various studies trying to determine the limits of what the human mind can survive. Psychologists have published a scale of stressors as a way of quantifying the effects and possible determination if someone is getting close to an emotional breakdown. In making those lists, some have argued which is the worst possible trauma: either a horrendous divorce where the person lives to keep hurting you, or the tragic loss of children topping the scale of the unbearable. Either way, the pain and darkness we personally experienced was mind-bending. Beyond that reality of pain and learning to cope, however, there are other more subtle things which we learned, and their power which I did not completely realize until one of them hit me with full force.

In late spring of 1995, we were visiting one of my aunts and joined her at her church. While we were sitting and listening to the preliminary activities leading up to the sermon, we were simply trying to relax in the beautiful environment before us. Then the pastor stood up to speak.

Moments into his presentation, he held up a horrible picture from the cover of a nationwide news magazine. It was one sliver of time captured with such power on film that it had lodged itself into the psyche of the American public. In fact, I am confident that as I describe it, you will readily remember the iconic picture.

As the pastor related the events of April 19, 1995, the visual in his hand captured me. The contrast of the bright red of the helmet and the yellow reflective lines of the uniform were unmistakable by design. They drew my eyes to see the object of the fireman's care in his arms: a little baby. The precious child's head was also red, but from blood. The child was not moving, like my children only four months previously, and the emergency personnel were unable to bring his little life back. The look on the fireman's face at that moment reflected the horror that ravaged my heart each day.

Standing behind the pulpit holding that picture before us, the pastor began to describe the horrendous events on the day of the Oklahoma City bombing. He moved from one scene to another in his mind's eye, obviously informed by quite a bit of reading, using eloquent language and powerful descriptions. He apparently was preparing to set the mood in order to teach something spiritual, though I cannot remember or comprehend now what it might have been.

The pastor went on in very specific detail to question what it must have been like for parents to drop their children off, relieved to be on time for daycare at the Alfred P. Murrah Building, and then never see them alive again. What would they remember? Had they fought that morning? Had they given them a hug, never realizing it would be their last? Regret would torment them the rest of their lives.

He contrasted it with a story of another family who happened to be running late that day. Perhaps they were late because things had not gone well, or quickly enough at their home. He imagined the roller coaster of emotions that that parent must have experienced: nagging and pushing their child to get ready, regret from possibly snapping at them in the process, speeding through traffic just to arrive minutes after the cataclysmic explosion, and then realizing their accumulated seconds of frustration had just spared their lives! The gasp of relief immediately subsuming whatever regret had been felt before.

The normal questions of why did this happen, along with impending judgment for perpetrators of such deeds may have finished the sermon, but I did not hear them. Weeping, uncontrollably, I was somewhere else. There in that sacred place of the church, I began to realize the difference small things can make. The look of love, a hug, a smile, snapped out commands, short exchanges, the unspoken words haunting your mind the rest of your life. Such monumental things these small experiences are when you're confronted by death.

Our experience in that church was by no means positive because of the pain it elicited from both Penny and me. However, later, it was truly enlightening. I don't believe we ever spoke with the pastor afterwards. I am sure we were not presentable. Maybe my aunt later went and talked with him to let him know what had happened because I am sure he could not have missed the spectacle of our weeping in the back of his church as he scanned the congregation while he spoke. He had done nothing wrong. It was an ignominious event, and one which created an opportunity to speak to some of the deepest challenges facing our society. How could he have known that in his church at that moment were parents who had recently lost their children? Later that afternoon when my tears subsided and my aunt had apologized profusely and repeatedly for such horrendous timing, I began reflecting.

The pastor was able to describe the situation and imagine the emotions with incredible and palpable sympathy. But I was actually *feeling* them! Unlike the pastor, going from eyewitness accounts which were written in the follow-up news articles, using his creative and emotional skills to capture and relay the feelings of that day, I relived those same emotions. As he recounted the inconsolable pain of those parents, I felt it.

I knew the pain of those parents who will live the rest of their lives recounting and replaying their final words. I lived the trauma and fear that comes with a loss like that. For me it was not simply information or sympathy, I experienced empathy.

In that moment I realized that the difference between sympathy and empathy is far more than a few little letters. It literally encompasses a gap that cannot be spanned without the additional alphabet of experience. It is one of the most powerful feelings one can have and share with another that connects their hearts together. It is not just knowing about something, or being able to describe facts, but to truly enter into it and know the depths of it. Though the details and times are always different, the person understands what is being shared. Empathy unites like no other experience.

Yet, in some mysterious twist of a God-directed destiny, empathy also empowers us.

Later in 1996, Penny and I had recovered enough that we were beginning to travel from church to church, preaching again. We had gotten more involved in young adult ministry. I especially liked "paintball evangelism"—shoot first, share God's love afterwards! While interacting with others we had learned that we had a story to share of God's grace (even before we knew what He was about to do in our lives later on).

One particular weekend we were ministering in a little country church. I stood in front of the small congregation and shared our story. At that time in our experience I was able to describe the beautiful picture of God's love that we were beginning to see. I actually think the title of the sermon was, Faith 201. We were students, so I was building on the system of class numbering that colleges use. A "100" level course is very general and goes over a wide range of topics at a shallow level whereas a "200" level course begins to go deeper into a smaller group. In my sermon I was suggesting that we were in the midst of learning about faith in God a little bit deeper. We were learning more than just the basic doctrines or details, but learning to actually begin to know God in the grind and pain of life.

I shared some of the examples of how the local church had so amazingly blessed Penny and me after the accident. I relayed the verses that had blessed us to that point. I finished the sermon with an emotional appeal to invite people to let God love them in the midst of whatever trials and troubles they were facing.

In that church as in many others, after closing prayer, the members file out the door shaking the speaker's hand. As I was shaking hands, meeting various people and listening to their heartfelt appreciation or habitual comment of gratitude that church was over (knowing lunch would follow), I looked ahead and saw a woman coming about six people away. Her eyes were locked onto me, and she seemed venomously angry.

Sensing she was coming towards me, I asked a nearby elder who she was. I was not prepared to be attacked that day. He looked at her, shrugged and told me she had recently lost her husband. I knowingly and gently nodded my head more to myself than anyone else because then I understood why she was angry.

As soon as she came near me I looked into her eyes and opened up my arms as I said the following words, "I just heard that you lost your husband. I am so sorry. I know our story must have hurt you horribly. Please forgive me."

I don't know whether it was my open arms, gentle voice, or the look on my face, but she collapsed into my arms, weeping. I held her and together we cried for a number of moments. Others may have felt awkward, but I knew the power of shared tears. Then, building on what we had learned from our own trauma and the fear of losing memories I asked her, "What was your husband's name?"

She lifted her head off of my shoulder with a beautiful smile. It was like she became a new person before my very eyes as she said his name. Her face began to glow as you could almost see her walking through decades of memories with her best friend. I continued to hold her as she shared her memories, and then I made a mistake and asked another question.

I asked, "Did your church love and treat you the way our church had loved us?"

Coiling her head back without warning the livid rage came back into her piercing eyes as she nearly spit out the answer, "No! Sure, they treated me a little differently for a few weeks—like I had the flu—but now they have forgotten!"

Oh, how my heart hurt for her as well as for her church. Hurt people *hurt* people!

Trying to recover, I encouraged her with the thought that maybe now after hearing our story they would do better. I hoped so, and I talked with the elders afterwards. I hope her story ended well.

So many of us are simply not prepared for, nor do we know how to love someone in the wake of the universal reality of pain and loss. We mean well. We don't want to hurt them more. My hope is that after reading about our story it will help us talk about the things that hurting people need because, normally, they will not tell you.

Nearly every holiday there are broken, lonely people sitting in most churches, weeping. Maybe they don't weep on the outside because they have learned that others don't understand, and they just don't know how to care. Or, maybe, they have simply become accustomed to being lonely in a crowd, maintaining their mask over their wounded hearts. Every gathering contains these people.

We pass one another on the streets, or sit next to them in waiting rooms. We work side-by-side, filtering our stories to maintain work relationships. We chase after community with cute pictures, short tweets, and fill our lives with activities, food, or chemicals in an attempt to outrun or numb our sorrows.

The palette of pain has many colors. Widows or widowers, alone, trying to cope without their best friend, and terrified for the future. Single parents reeling from a lost or toxic relationship, struggling to survive and give their children hope for another day. Young people with dashed dreams, trying to find their place in life while fighting off a myriad of addictions which line up to dash more dreams. Families traumatized by a visit to the doctor's office. Refugees stripped of their lives, running to try to find another. Professionals trying to live the life their work and the public requires of them, all the while rotting and eroding from the inside out. There are no easy answers in the face of so many combinations of pain.

Enter empathy.

Could it be the discussion about why "bad things happen to good people" is not actually a question about God, but is more of a question for us? Maybe it is more about our self-centered focus which blinds us to the world around us, and pain is the tool which turns our eyes towards others? It is not God's lack of interest, goodness, or power that allows the pain. Could it be, in fact, His creative (even re-creative) genius that allows some of us to experience the dregs of pain, letting us become so saturated in as many colors as possible so that in time, and with His incredible healing love, we are equipped to connect and recognize that same pain in others?

Shared empathy recognizes the masks, and invites others to be real in their pain, in order to allow the same hope that has moved *us* forward to hold and bless *them* as well. When we let Him love us in the midst of whatever path is before us, God can use all the colors of pain to form a human masterpiece of grace.

The question comes down to this: will you let God bring you through the pain so you can bless the world around you?

Forgiveness

We must develop and maintain
the capacity to forgive.
He who is devoid of the power to forgive
is devoid of the power to love.
There is some good in the worst of us
and some evil in the best of us.
When we discover this,
we are less prone to hate our enemies.

Martin Luther King, Jr.

It took nearly sixteen years. I would never have imagined it could take that long. Maybe my lack of empathy made it actually impossible for me to comprehend what was happening. I was baffled. What made this struggle even more difficult was that it was out of my control. I could say the right words, I could encourage, I could pray and hope, but I could not do it. I could not help my wife do what she needed to do.

This was my amazing Penny, who in December of 2001 had joined me in a calling to take our two miracle children, Elijah and Hannah, ages four and three, to go and serve the Muslim minority people in Cambodia in a post 9/11 world. She was willing to sell everything we owned and take our precious children halfway around the globe to live with people we did not know, people who quite possibly did not even want to have an American family living in their village. She had pushed herself to stomach new foods, experience exotic tropical bugs, both inside and outside of our bodies. She had pushed herself to wrap her tongue and brain around learning an ancient, challenging language, and to precariously hang onto motorcycles with two children and only one working hand. She let her husband travel around the country visiting mosques and Muslims in their homes, knowing that probably everybody was eyeing him suspiciously as either a missionary, CIA operative, or *both*! She had followed me in a life so far outside of her comfort zone I simply thought she could do anything.

But not this.

Some wounds take a long time to heal. If infected, they never heal. The process of cleaning wounds can cause great pain. Other times breaks in bones need to be re-broken and reset. Such is the reality with our body. But what about our emotions?

Along with the aspect of choice and time allowing torn emotions to mend, are there other things which need to be rooted out to allow for full healing? Fear, betrayal and injustice immediately come to mind as some of the grit and dirt that often infect and delay the healing process. Each of those are emotions and wounds that come from without, usually from someone or something else. They are certainly painful when you pull them out, work on cleaning the wound and then identify the external object which continues to hurt you. But there is another wound which is internal, and much more difficult to deal with.

Blame.

This pathogen is everywhere. We give it to each other and allow it to continually mutate and multiply in our own minds. Words can carry it in the wind. Movies and billboards invoke it. It can be as simple as a look which implies the failure or judgment of someone else. It is in the constant nagging feeling of not measuring up or not owning the "right" stuff. It's blaming yourself or someone else for your pain. Untreated, there is no healing for this infection. Most of the time we can deal with blame from the outside by realizing that what is expected or being "sold" to us is ridiculous, or we can talk to enough people to properly quarantine it and file it away in order for it to no longer affect us. When people say things or judge us it may still hurt deeply for awhile, but in the end, the blame is deemed impotent and we go on.

This was my experience when we had to make the very difficult decision to leave Cambodia. Our hearts were knit together with so many other broken Cambodians who had been devastated by the regime of Pol Pot and the Khmer Rouge. Our eyes could see their pain. Our shared empathy spoke a language above words. Though very challenging, our time there had been one rich with growth.

However, within a year and-a-half of our arrival in Cambodia we became acutely aware of the prejudice against Elijah due to his skin color being darker than the local culture. Everywhere Penny went she had to deal with people inappropriately touching, hugging, or praising Hannah, all the while ignoring, hurting, or mocking Elijah. They would even tell her in Khmae, "You have a beautiful white daughter and an ugly black son!" As Elijah's language skills began to grow she could see him literally wilting as the comprehension of their words and actions pelted him day after day.

In order to save both Elijah and Hannah from that toxic environment, we decided we had to leave. Though we tried, we could not change the culture, and the perceptions of race and adoption were viral. In the process of choosing to protect our children who we knew God had given to us, some work colleagues said I was betraying my calling and even turning my back on God by leaving before our allotted time was up. Some even sliced me with the scalpel of Scripture, severing ties and leaving me wounded from their spiritual malpractice.

I experienced self-blame. I felt the piercing judgments and implied failure. It hurt for a long time! But, in the end, I realized I had made the right choice and the imposed blame dissolved, eventually healing over with only the scar remaining.

I am sure in my experience, part of that self-blame was effectively disproved when Penny became pregnant again and gave birth to a healthy boy, Noah, within a year of our return to the United States in 2004. Noah was another unplanned miracle, and I sensed that he was like a confirmation from God. In my mind, since we had stood for our family, God was once again blessing us with another precious child.

But for Penny there was still an untouched tumor. Her self-blame seemed malignant.

Although no one ever implied it, or even dared to say it (apart from one insurance agent speaking out of turn in an inhumane way), the unspoken stalked her.

Was it her fault that Caleb and Abigail were dead? Had she caused them to die early? Tortured, she feverishly fought with the twin indicators of blame: "why?" and "what if?" How had she failed them? Was it her fault?

Even when she overcame her daunting fears associated with driving, and victoriously received her license again in 2004, guilt, like an autoimmune disease, lurked beneath the surface. Something more had to free her of this infection.

Like an attending physician seeking to limit the spread of certain symptoms, God prescribed some long-term medications of grace and love to work in her for a few years. In her personal times of worship, as she read about a God of grace and mercy, He seemed to sit close to her, like a caring surgeon, outlining the steps ahead in the plan for her recovery and wholeness. He is the God who seeks us in our brokenness and holds us in our pain. Slowly her pain lessened as she believed that she could still be loved, and that she was not being blamed for the accident. The whispers of God's goodness and grace, like the steady drip of medicine in an IV, slowly raised her defenses against the attacks of depression and self-blame. God's assurances that her life mattered and that she was still valuable targeted the viruses. Words of truth and value slowly undermined the lies of blame.

I am sure more symptoms dissipated when she became pregnant yet again in late 2006. Eight months later, as she held our fourth child, little Hadassah Grace, even more healing ensued. It seemed God was clearly smiling on Penny's role as a mother with the repeated blessings which whispered both exoneration and affirmation.

Each successful trip with her four children in the car further bolstered her courage and gave her hope that one day she would be free from her inappropriate feelings of blame and failure. She celebrated many small victories such as properly parking in a busy lot, or even following the moving van and not getting lost while going to the home God provided for us in Covington, Georgia, in 2007.

Every miracle of His mercy added to her sense of confidence to go forward in the face of the disease. But she was not cured. To be completely cured she seemed to need an injection of something much more powerful. In 2010, another experience painfully pierced our world, and was the means of delivering that medicine.

We were traveling home from some meetings as a family and stopped at a gas station in Virginia in the midst of a snow storm. I rested in the van while Penny and Noah briefly went inside. Afterwards, as they were walking back through the parking lot, a woman hit and nearly backed over them with her car, never stopping or looking back to see what had happened. Within moments our world was rocked again.

I did not see the whole thing, but the woman was eventually found. Let me share with you the letter we later wrote to the woman who could have killed our little Noah and maimed Penny. The letter was given to the lawyer the day before the lady's trial for the hit and run. Due to her record and some other details in her life, she was potentially facing felony charges and prison.

June 10, 2010 at 3:16pm

Dear Lady,

This is a strange letter to write. I hope it will mean something to you. I don't know how these things work and whether or not you will be able to read this and if so, when. But, I want to share some things with you, hoping that they may prove to be a blessing to you someday.

Tomorrow I am required to testify against you regarding the day you hit my son and me with your car. I don't want to testify. I want to forgive.

I do forgive you. But, that forgiveness is not flippantly nor freely given just because it sounds good. It is said with real awareness of what could have been.

I have buried children before. When you hit Noah and me on that afternoon, my mind was flooded with the memories of nearly sixteen years ago when our two precious ones died in a car accident back in Wisconsin. Fear gripped my heart as I saw Noah bleeding from his head and I simply did not know what to do next. Your actions that day opened up old wounds that don't heal easily.

But, I still choose to forgive.

I don't know what you were
thinking when you left the scene.
Obviously when you hit us you were
not doing it with any malicious
intent. Accidents happen, and it was
a horrible mistake. Maybe it was a
phone call, or the snow, or simply
not looking back enough. Either way,
accidents happen, mistakes happen.
Oh, how we know that and have been
broken through them before.

But, why did you leave? Our son
could have been killed from that head
injury. He could have fallen beneath
your car—praise God Almighty he
did not.

Yet, you did not even stop to see,
to care what had happened.

Maybe you were scared, maybe
you didn't know—though the
witnesses said they told you and tried
to stop you. Maybe. . . ?

I don't understand. My
mother heart cannot even begin to
comprehend how you could leave and
add such a horrible choice to such
a mistake.

But, I still choose to forgive.

My little boy was terrified as
he was taken to the hospital in the
ambulance. I was horrified to be in
an ambulance again and it brought
back the painful realities of when my
first two children died. I was so afraid

he was never going to see again. My
precious little Noah who loves life so
much, losing his eye! What horrible
fear! That day reopened a chasm of
pain in my life.

I praise God that Noah's eye was
not permanently damaged and that
he is okay. My leg is fine. But we did
not know that on that afternoon, and
had to carry that fear and pain of not
knowing the future. It was a miracle
that we weren't hurt more than we
were. God's hand was upon us to keep
us from falling under your vehicle.
God turned what could have been a
tragic day into a day of reflection,
grace, mercy, and praise, as He kept
us safe.

In light of all those realities,
I still choose to forgive.

As I am choosing to forgive, I am
also wondering and praying for you.
What was going through your mind?
What is going through your thoughts
right now?

I don't know what the State will
do or how they will pursue things. I
wish there was another way and my
husband and I are praying that through
this horrible time for you that God will
use it to bless you in the long run.

I don't know what else to say. I
don't know how things are supposed to
work in legal issues like this.

You may be facing some pretty serious consequences ahead. Maybe these words will mean nothing to the prosecutor or judge, but we hope they will mean something to you, no matter how this next day unfolds.

We (my husband and I) hope that through this situation, and the grace which has been given to us will roll over into your life as well, like a healing tidal wave of mercy. Mercy received and mercy given. May you hear from the words of this note that we don't hold this against you. The State may still do what it will do. But, from the human to human level, and the God-directed realities that are available to us because of His love, we are choosing to forgive.

We hope that those words will give you hope and call you to a better set of choices. Choices to forgive (even yourself) and to move on. Choices to make the best of each day given to you (wherever they may be in the future). Choices.

Choices matter. Choices can reset things. On that afternoon you made a horrible, even life changing (almost ending) mistake followed by a choice. We hope and pray through this letter and our heartfelt prayers for you now, that you will make a life changing (life giving) choice to give your choices to

God, stop running from your previous poor choices, and live the rest of your days with a purpose and desire to make the world a better place for your being in it.

We choose to forgive. We know God forgives you, too. We hope this note will help you forgive yourself.

Sincerely,

Penny & Bryan

Did you see it? In writing the letter and experiencing its words, Penny was set free from her cancerous captor! That day Penny was healed. When she finally accepted and shared God's forgiveness, her blame dissolved.

Only the antidote of forgiveness can counteract the poison of blame. No one is perfect. Everyone needs to be forgiven, and God has already made that possible. God knows our needs. He completely knows our mistakes and completely accepts us. The love is there. There is nothing we can do to make Him love us less, and there is nothing we can do to make Him love us more. When we realize the unimaginable truth of His forgiveness, we are cured.

Yet, the full power of forgiveness is only truly actuated when it is given to another. It heals us in the transferring of it to someone else. Then, when that time of healing fully matures we are like survivors of the Ebola virus, and our blood carries the antibodies so we can serve the world offering more forgiveness.

Forgiven people forgive people! The cycle is contagious.

Identity

The greatest thing you'll ever learn
is just to love
and be loved in return.

Nat King Cole

In 2009 I was invited to go to Kazakhstan and share a series of presentations to help equip local Christians to become more willing and able to connect with the Muslim community. The leaders there recognized that simply doing what they had always done would not bridge the ever-widening gap between their communities.

At the time I was leading a nonprofit work called Enoch's Passion which focused on inviting people into a deeper walk with God regardless of their religion. Based largely on the powerful picture of God from our personal story, our experiences living immersed in a Muslim setting in Cambodia, and finishing my degree in Islamic Studies, I was often called to go to various places around the world as a spiritual bridge person who attempted to bring groups together in positive ways.

Both then and now we live in a world where it seems people are being polarized. Long ago humanity was denuded of our dignity as loved children of God, and in its place we have fashioned many gross coverings, patchwork labels trying to deny or cover our shame. Instead of accepting our identity in God and seeing individuals for who they are created to be, unique in their stories yet similar in the shared journeys of life, we judge and segregate according to a myriad of differences. Often, groups use God to defend their views and they're known more for what they're against rather than what they are for.

My main message invites people to see what they have in common and to grow together in a shared journey of worship to God, how to find their unique beauties, and how to unite in service to their community. I believe faith in God should bring out the best in us, not the worst! What good is anyone's religion if it does not result in blessing those around them?

Arriving in Almaty, I enjoyed the change of scenery from the United States. This was an awe-inspiring country with its backdrop of sentry mountains. The architecture surprised me with its variety of different cultures all coming together in one place: Russian, Middle Eastern, Modern, Eastern, and the various historic sites chronicling years past. Like the wind, it was a brisk and refreshing week.

In one of my introductory talks I shared facets of my story of devastation and pain. Recounting the aspects of our slow and painful journey through grief, I could see the telltale scars in others' eyes. Pain is a universal language.

I related the tangible ways our friends had blessed us. I explained how our old and warped pictures needed to change as we let God's love set us free. Quoting the verses from Jeremiah 31:3 and 29:11, I pointed out God's undeniable actions in our lives and the evidence of His fingerprints in the births of Elijah and Hannah. Then, building on the fact that this God of love is the God with a plan, there came a twist. In the years following the accident God had not only loved us and guided us, but He had also given us back four children when before there were only two! I added the next powerful reality: this same God of love is also the God with the power to turn everything for good: "And we know that all things work together for good to those who love God, to those who are the called according to His purpose." Romans 8:28

Scanning the group I could see these three simple verses were creating a whole new way of thinking in light of my testimony. Of course, this is not a blanket approval of all the pain and suffering in the world. Sometimes people make choices to fight against what is best for them and suffer many things because of it. If we break obvious laws of science and life, God will not normally protect us from those consequences. Yet, even after that "rebellion" against ourselves, responding to God's love allows His plan and power to turn it all, still, for good! I cannot explain this but have seen it in my own life. God is faithful!

Noting their intense focus, I built on the possibilities of what life might look like if we actually believed those three principles and oriented our lives towards God's will instead of warring against it.

First, we would no longer be afraid for our lives. We would be able to rest in the knowledge that we are loved and cared for, come what may. We would realize that whatever enters our lives is actually allowed by

God's design to bless and change us. One of the things I have learned is that God's plan for us is not just for our short lives here on earth but what we have been created for: eternity. His plan is not necessarily for our temporary comfort, but is for our eternal character. When we realize that, everything changes. We are able to see every circumstance and challenge in our life as an opportunity, allowed or crafted by God to bless us in the end.

The second obvious implication, if we truly believed this is that we would be more bold with our lives. We would no longer be shackled with a fear of what people think about us, because we already know we are loved and accepted. We would not be driven frantically from one situation to another trying to care for ourselves, afraid of failure, when we realize that we are already provided for and have been given promises of abundance. We would be filling whatever lot we might find ourselves in life to the best of our ability, trusting that God is guiding and using it to bless us.

One more evidence of these beliefs becoming reality: we would be free to truly love people. We would no longer worry about, and could be free from wearing masks in order to try to keep people thinking that we are acting a certain way, or trying to prop up our value before their eyes. Our identity would be anchored in our position as God's children instead of on our performance in a world of actors!

Imagine being fully known and fully loved by God like that! Then imagine being set free to love the world around us. What a glorious way of living!

I remember as I closed off that worshipful time with the group that some were crying, others were notably moved, and still others had taken copious notes. I could see that their minds were mulling over this new way of thinking and living. I was blessed by the power of that moment, went on with my other teaching commitments, and finished off my week there.

Just before I was going to leave on the last night, something happened which brought me to one more important lesson of what it means to be loved like this. My translator came with a woman to where I was sitting in the back of another meeting.

My translator related how her friend had been listening when I shared the previous worship time and was very angered by it! She did not believe what I was saying could even be true. Therefore, my translator asked me if I would be willing to talk with her about that.

Of course, I was happy to talk with her, and was intrigued to know why she was angry with what I had shared. That began a three-way conversation with the translator doing double-duty in two languages. Within a few moments it became obvious we needed to have more time together, and in a more private place. We excused ourselves from the back of the meeting room and went to find another room.

The woman was angry about what I had said because she had lost her husband nearly two years prior. She was in horrendous pain. She felt abandoned by her husband due to his death, and now had to raise her four children alone. When he died she was immediately surrounded by fear of the unknown and their future, the overwhelming responsibility of having to provide for her children, and the never-ending questions as to why God would allow her husband to die. In fact, it was so overwhelming that she did not even accept it.

She didn't believe her husband was dead! Almost every day she would still see him somewhere in the crowd, in a taxi, on a bus, somewhere away from her. From the corner of her eye her mind kept catching a glimpse of him, expecting him to come home eventually. Even though friends had told her over and over that he would not be coming home, that he was dead, she was literally locked in a world of denial.

Each night her children would go to bed crying out, needing her care, and yet she was unable to offer it. After two years many people would have begun to go forward with life, yet she was still locked in a painful cycle of depression and denial. Her children needed her, but she was barely functioning.

I listened to her story with a broken heart. Although I have not experienced the loss of a spouse and am not completely aware of the additional nuances of grief that that brings, I do know the pain of death. We all wept freely as she told her story and I asked questions, trying to understand. The lone box of tissues failed to keep us dry.

I was amazed as I saw my translator friend reaching out and caring for her friend with such deep love. Her mind must have been going at unspeakable speeds in order for her to have been able to have been a human bridge connecting these two people before her. With compassion she would see the emotion and listen to the gut-wrenching story of her friend, and then communicate those words in another language as best she could.

Some of the words she did not even need to translate because my heart already understood. Empathy transcends language. We spent more than an hour listening to her share her pain and her anger with God.

I understood. I have no need to defend God. For one, He is big enough to defend Himself. Second, there are things I do not understand, and I have many of my own questions for God. I assured her my testimony did not mean that I no longer had questions for Him. In the course of my own story what *had* changed was my perspective that God is bigger than I can contain. I do not understand Him, but I can worship what I see. I do not control Him, but I can trust Him to be good. I do not have all the answers, but I can trust Him to be faithful in the journey.

The simple and painful act of listening to her express her anger and raw emotion was an exhausting event. Each of us was wrung out as the first hour moved over for the second to take its place.

One thing I have noticed in the years since our accident is that grieving people say horrible things. When someone is hurting, the mouth becomes a weapon to empty the ready emotional arsenal at anyone within target range. She was no exception. As her visceral emotions began to explode from deep within, the machine gun of the mouth took aim against God, the church, people, and life itself. All I could do was hold her hand and weep, doing my best emotionally to dodge as many of the projectiles flying in the general vicinity of me. It was very difficult. I know I'm not God's shield, but there is such a tendency to want to defend Him and have all the answers.

After she was able to express her pain and trauma, she eventually settled down enough and paused. Because I had honored her by listening and not defended or corrected her, her heart expressed relief. Exhausted, she was open to listen a little.

I was able to share, in agreement with her horrendous pain, some of the experiences my wife and I had endured. I told her how my wife had found such incredible comfort in a verse in the book of Psalms 56:8, where God says He keeps a record of our tears in a bottle. As those words were translated I could see her eyes responding with a look of relief, as though she was being invited to just fall into the ever-patient arms of God, knowing that He understood her pain and would remember.

We spent more than two hours together working through her questions, but not necessarily finding answers. The simple act of listening is sometimes all that we can do. The shared camaraderie of the suffering is an unspoken bond.

In our time together she moved from being an angry, hurting person into a place where she was beginning to realize that God's love was inviting her forward. Her very face had changed. I could sense the key of acceptance turning in the door of her heart to set her free from the prison of grief she had been locked in for so long. I know that dark place.

Then something happened. I cannot completely explain it, but I can describe it. A black cloud seemed to slide across the space between us, like a guard pushing the prisoner back into the dungeon. Clearly, something else was in the room at that moment. Her face contorted and she went back into her locked, angry disposition, and she began to vehemently attack God again.

In a split second, welling up deep from within me, came a righteous boldness that burst forth against whatever that new black presence was. I spoke with power and authority in the name of God and in the name of truth, that this woman was in the act of being set free. Almost like a young boy trying to contain the overpowering force of a fireman's hose I could not direct nor control the words that were flowing out of me. Verses of Scripture in rapid succession battered away at the intruder. The translator's voice matched the speed and intensity of mine as we went to war for our sister. Whatever was trying to cloud her world, in the name of God, we fought it off.

It didn't take very long. In just moments the surreal event was over. Peace rested on her face. My mind returned to its normal state of self-control. All three of us sat in silent amazement. Another captive had been set free!

Hours later while flying back across the ocean I reflected on what had happened. Recounting the events of that night I was stunned. My thoughts turned into a prayer.

Oh God! What would it be like if we truly trusted Your love? What heights of compassion could we reach if we no longer feared for our future, knowing it was in His hands? With what bold authority would we confront the darkness and lies enslaving our brothers and sisters if we knew He could turn everything for good? What would change if we lived our lives knowing who we are, and Whose we are? True authority is always tied to our concept of identity. How would we live out our inheritance as children of God, where our every desire was simply to see love and truth rush over the world like a tidal wave of grace and goodness?

My prayers drifted off into a dream.

What a dream!

Salvation

O Lord, if I worship You
because of fear of hell
then burn me in hell.
If I worship You because I desire paradise
then exclude me from paradise.
But if I worship You for Yourself alone
then deny me not Your eternal beauty.

Rabia Basri

One morning in 2010 I had a dream. I clearly saw one of my classmates from my University of Georgia days where we were both working on our Islamic Studies Masters degree. Hanafi was a Fulbright scholar from Indonesia and we had become close friends, seeing each other every day until he left in 2006. It was great to see him again in my dream. I decided to pray for him, as I do whenever I recognize someone in my dreams, asking God to bless him wherever he might be at that moment. The day went on and I did not think about it again until my phone rang.

From out of the blue, a stranger was calling to ask me to consider moving my family to Indonesia to begin an interfaith study center in the hope of trying to connect Muslims and Christians together. I was dumbfounded as I listened. On exactly the same day that I had dreamt of Hanafi, I was being asked to go and live in the largest Muslim-populated country in the world!

As I shared the conversation and the "coincidence" of the dream with my wife, we immediately recognized the distinct style of God inviting us to take another crazy walk with Him! We jokingly, yet seriously, tell people we have learned to walk "blind." God has never failed us! Months later, and after many more growing experiences, we uprooted, and moved to another country, preparing to be outsiders again, and to let God show us more of His goodness. What an adventure!

The next three and-a-half years were filled with so many more lessons that I will one day write them down in another book. It seemed to be a time of deployment for us. It was an opportunity to build on the things God had proven to, and taught, us. It was an opportunity to give us a platform to break down the walls of ignorance and prejudice, and then invite both Christians and Muslims into a life of peace and purpose.

Building on the shared goodness and characteristics of the God of Abraham worshipped by all of the monotheistic faiths, we witnessed the beginning of a movement. People of faith choosing to agree on the worship of the One, True God, and to live their lives fully surrendered to Him and committed to being a blessing in the world. Watching God coordinate events and people into one direction like that was awe-inspiring. We watched the work we began in Indonesia continue to unite people in a journey of blessing to the world around them.

In my position in creating a study center, I was privileged to travel and speak all over the country and Southeast Asia. I was even reunited with my dear brother, Hanafi, a few times in East Java. Those were rich years of growth and blessings as I learned to share simple, powerful messages and illustrations that could survive translation.

This is one of my favorite illustrations when I find myself in front of people who might be considered conservative or very religious, whether they are Christian or Muslim. In circles such as these there is one all-consuming question which is answered in different ways. The question in one form or another is: are you saved?

It is a question often asked by or to hitchhikers within the first minute of entering a vehicle in the Bible Belt of the United States. Other times and places the query is not with words, but by the glances Muslims sometimes give a new person entering their mosque. The response to this question (uttered or not), is used to course the direction of any future conversation, or for setting the feelings of assumed security. It is, again, the human tendency to want to compare ourselves with others and to make a judgment call which helps us to feel better about ourselves. Or, it is used to determine if we have things in common. Ironically, the question should bring peace to the heart and closer relationships, yet it often brings war to the world.

Knowing this, I have regularly had fun by asking a related question designed to cause trouble. In case you were wondering, sometimes being free in your identity causes a warped sense of adventure and humor since you become accustomed to letting God lead and pull you out of (or into) crazy situations! I will ask a simple question and then wait awhile before following it with my answer. Sometimes I need to adjust the words a little to make sure they fit the context, but I ask the same question regardless of the group, whether Muslim, Christian, or mixed. The gist of it is this:

"Do you know when you were saved?"

For some groups they do not know, and even teach that one cannot know, and therefore, by letting God determine the answer, live in uncertainty of the future. Some people in certain groups pride themselves on the exact day, moment or sermon which moved them from the darkness into the light. Still, other groups sit anxiously quiet because as much as they want to know, they simply don't. There are even some which would be distracted by the implication of the question being in the past. As I ask the question, I let my listeners respond in various ways or squirm in the uneasiness of the feelings associated with this metaphysical quagmire. Then I give my answer.

"God saved me when my children died before my very eyes!"

Silence.

You hear the proverbial pins dropping around the room.

Obviously, I don't smile when I say that because I cannot rejoice in that reality. This answer sets up confusion since salvation should be a joyful thing. As the words begin to connect in the ears of my listeners, confusion begins to overtake the crowd. Faces crumple as they ponder the incongruity of the picture. How on earth could the death of my children save me? This seems to be a contradiction of terms.

Then, when I know I have everyone's attention, as these thoughts are assaulting every aspect of the audiences' religious traditions, I explain what I mean.

What I mean is that God saved me from my warped picture of Him, and began to set me free to a completely different life on the day my children died. God was able to take an unspeakable act and turn it for good. In the ensuing darkness, in the shadows of the months that followed our accident, God saved me!

He broke me free from a life of comparing myself with others or with an unattainable list. He liberated me from a schizophrenic fear that I could never measure up to everyone's standards, even His. My understanding of faith changed from being able to explain God, or defend Him, to simply being able to trust Him.

He saved me from a life of random hopelessness and gave me an incredible purpose. He moved me from futility to focus. My life no longer depends upon what other people think of me because I know I am completely known and loved by God. I could no longer be satisfied with a self-centered, minuscule existence of petty entertainment. I wanted to become all I could be and experience life at its fullest, growing each and every day. My self-esteem was no longer connected with my performance, but was anchored in my position as a created and redeemed child of God. I am no longer a slave to my past. I am free to live and love forever! Each day is now pregnant with hope and purpose as I am privileged to participate in the grand scheme of God loving others in me, through me, and often, even in spite of me!

More than my pictures of Him and my understanding of myself, God also saved my marriage. By forcing my wife and me to start over, God delivered us. In our pain and brokenness, when we could do nothing in our own strength, God gave us patient friends and books, like *Love and Respect* by Emerson Eggerichs, which taught us what the commitment to love entailed, and how to use proper communication to nurture our relationship. As we chose to love again, and learned how to stop fighting *with* each other and began to fight *for* each other, we experienced the beauty of marriage as it is intended to be. He saved us.

God also saved my amazing Penny, who before was so fragile and wounded when I had courted and married her in a rush of testosterone immaturity years ago. She is now the most tremendous woman of faith and resilience I am privileged to know! I am privileged to see her through the years of her overcoming never-ending nerve pain in her arm, regular headaches, having to always protect her left hand from being burned because there is no more sensory perception, to the incomprehensible loss of her three children constantly calling her to despair, and through the mental warfare against the years of toxic self-talk from the abused brokenness of her early home life. Through each of these trials God had sustained her and transformed her. God had used powerful authors such as Joyce Meyer and Ellen White to make scripture speak a language Penny could hear. But, more than information and truth, Penny has *fought* to be who she is.

In addition to her fighting to become who she is, personally, God has also been using her to bless many young women who have lived with us throughout the years. Just in the course of our living in Indonesia for the last three and-a-half years she has opened up our home to more than ten girls. For one semester we actually had seven at once! Imagine that, every meal was cooked for more than ten people! We literally ate up our salary.

When the estrogen level and noise got too high I would escape to my little bamboo prayer hut in the backyard with the chickens and geese for some alone time. Sitting there staring at the majestic mountain behind us, hearing the regular call to prayer reverberating all around me, I would recharge and pray. In the soul-quiet that re-orients what is important, I gained glimpses of the way God was using Penny to mold future wives and mothers who would impact that country for years to come.

Yet, there is one more way in which God saved me on December 3, 1994. In addition to changing me, my view of Him, my wife, my marriage, my purpose in life, and giving me a family again, there was still the need to save me from my view of the world. In the past I had seen others and the world around me through the eyes of fear. Actually, I would never have admitted that it was fear. I would have called it "discernment" or, "judgment." I would categorize and label people according to many social, religious, and historic constructs, all in an effort to maintain my value, to know where I fitted in. Yet, underneath all of that was fear, fear of who they might be, what they might do to me, fear of them changing what I believed or who I thought I was.

Facing the ultimate thing to be afraid of, death, and watching God turn and use it all for good changes you. There are still momentary reflex responses to physical dangers, but the deep paralysis of the paradigm of fear has been broken. God's love and power has set me free.

I can now see people for who they are and enjoy being with them without judgment. I see them through the eyes of love. I invite you to look back over your life and see if there are places where God has tried to break through and set you free. This is hard for many to see because often-times we use religion, wealth, fame, or power to prop up our value, and to maintain the external façade of our faces and our faith. There is even an insidious lie being promoted around the world that if you are faithful to God, or good at what you do, or who you are, then only good things will come your way. That is often the furthest from the truth. Bad things happen to good people. The world is a messy and tormented place.

Yet, even in the messiness, I have learned that as we grow deeper in our understanding of God, the bad can come, and we learn to trust Him in the midst of the storm. The greatest gems can only be created through tremendous pressure and time. God allows us to be broken, re-formed, pushed, and crushed at times, so our lives will reveal the glorious fragrance or unseen beauty we were created to share with a world of wounded people. The longer I live, and the more miracles I see of God's power to turn all things for good, I believe one of God's greatest trusts is suffering! In a world of horrendous pain and sin He prepares some children who will let Him work in the fiery trials of their lives so that later they can be prepared to bless others in spite of, and through their trials. Such a life is the ultimate, ironic salvation which no one would willingly volunteer for, yet in the end, when they see the way God can use it for His glory, transforming them and the world around them, they would not choose otherwise!

So, let me ask you, "When were you saved?"

Epilogue

In the years that have followed the accident, our lives have continued to unfold in a series of miraculous experiences that defy explanation. I like to say that miracles can become the new normal when we walk in the life God is inviting us to. I have tasted just a little of it and I want more!

In wanting more, God keeps leading us farther and farther into the unknown. Every challenge simply becomes a chance for God to show His power again. The war is learning to surrender our wills and trust Him to fight for us instead of our desire to do it ourselves. The battle is more inside than out! The moment we surrender and trust, He turns it for good. Living that way, life can literally go from victory to victory!

Whenever I travel and speak, regardless of the location or the country, there is a regular comment that is made. I understand why people make it and I am grateful to know God's grace is touching hearts as they are moved to say such things. I have found that the same answer continues to well up from within my heart when I respond. It is not meant to be a flippant answer even though it kind of rolls off of my tongue.

The comment usually comes as they look at my life and see the way in the years since the accident that

God has so incredibly blessed my wife and me. He has taken us from a place of brokenness and the unspeakable horror of burying our two children, to giving us four more children in a nearly miraculous fashion, and leading us to live a life of purpose, peace, passion and power in a world that rarely sees that.

So the comment makes sense from those who know the historic allusion to which it is being referred. But I have felt the need to answer as I do, because the comment is built upon an inappropriate comparison. My answer is a way of moving people to see the bigger picture.

You are probably trying to figure out what on earth is that particular statement. I understand. I wanted to give you time to think about it a little bit first.

The comment people make almost every single time I speak and share our story is something along the lines of "You are a modern-day Job," or, "You are like Job," and other possible statements connecting my name with that great prophet of old.

I understand why they're making the statement. There are some obvious connections with my losing two children and now having four, and apparently they see our now-changed faith remains. The connections break down in the area of animals because I am a little short on the livestock and camels Job received, but maybe they will come later! Still, the comparison is understandable.

When I hear this over and over, my answer is very intentional. I suppose you could say it serves as a protection against pride. But it's always important for me and my human nature to appropriately deflect and refocus with this answer:

"I am not Job.

But, the God of Job still lives!"

I want people to realize it's not about the human tendency to compare or measure pain and blessings received, and rank who is the "best" faith-filled person. Instead, it is realizing that the One whom we need to trust is *still there*.

The love, faithfulness, guidance in the midst of the darkest places—all of these attributes of our omnipotent God remain. God is where our focus and our faith must be. Not in ourselves or our works (good or bad), but in His faithfulness.

The purpose for telling this story is so that it will change both me and you. It is to empower us to trust God fully through whatever comes our way.

What will that mean for your future life? What will it look like in mine? Those details and answers remain to be seen.

It has been just over twenty years since the day that transformed our lives. So much has changed. I know there is much more to come, and whatever it may hold for my family, we will choose to receive it graciously knowing this: the God of love is the God with the plan, and He is also the God with the power to turn everything for good. Because of that amazing love and mercy in our lives, I invite you to open your heart to this God whose faithfulness is truly, without question, undeniable.

Contact Information

Some of my deepest friendships and most sublime thoughts have been connected with books. I hope that this one will bless you in a similar way.

If you would like to share any comments or begin a conversation about how *Undeniable* has affected you, please contact me at *http://Undeniablethebook.com.*

Design Notes

How is depth of emotion translated into a graphic that not only represents feeling, but draws one into the experience?

The strength of this story brought to mind the flowers that respond to the sun even while buried below the snow. Research showed that the Lenten Rose (Helleborus) thrives in shade and blooms when other plants are not even awake yet.

As every plant, Lenten Roses bud, slowly open, and finally bloom with faces seeking the sun. So the graphics in this book make the journey of resurrection along with the story.

The lines around the graphics also have meaning. In the first section there is a complete box, yet section by section the lines fall away until that closure becomes a single foundation line, again following the message of *Undeniable*.

Acknowledgments

A project like this cannot be done well by one person, and certainly not me! I am indebted to so many, both in our actual journey up to this point, and also in the process of telling this amazing story. It is so easy to say "thank you," yet merely enunciating those two words fails to capture the true depth of their meaning. In my thanks to God, I can offer my life in praise and adoration for all that He has done. Yet, to thank people I will have to rely on my feeble words at this time.

Immediately my mind turns to my precious wife and children. Penny, in many ways, you are both my inspiration and motivation to share this story. You are amazing. Thank you for your support and encouragement to finish this book. Without your sacrificing and being willing to carry the load with the family many times as I wrote, this book would not be a reality. Elijah, your crystal clear observation about the cover made it better. Thank you for being an ongoing source of blessing to us. Hannah, even though you and Elijah have been away at school for much of the writing, your design comments, phone calls and editorial help have made this book a beautiful and powerful testimony of our story. It has been a lot of fun working together and I hope we can collaborate on more books in the future. I'm so blessed to be the Dad of such awesome teenagers. I love you both! Noah and Hadassah, you have sacrificed your daddy time to make this book possible. Though you did not necessarily choose to let me go and write, and I know you were sad as the days stacked up, it was your smiles and hugs when I returned which kept pushing me forward to finish well. One day, I hope the words of this book will bless you too, knowing just how grateful we are that you are in our lives!

Throughout this book I have mentioned many people who have helped us in this journey. Thank you, from the bottom of our hearts for all you have done to bless us. Our story would be completely different without you and your love. No words can adequately express our gratitude.

As this is my first book, I have had to learn many things, and I needed patient editors and a designer to walk me through the process. Jan, Rachel and Ardie, I am so grateful for your help, kindness, and professional care. Your collective balance of precision and encouragement urged me forward and has resulted in an unforgettable book.

I also want to say a big thank you to Greg, Ivanna, Jannah, Judy and Rhoda for being willing to read the unfinished manuscript and share valuable insight to help me finish it.

This book might never have left the confines of my mind if it weren't for places of quiet and solitude needed to write it. My sincere thanks to Brian for letting me escape to the lake house and write for days on end. The silence was exactly what I needed. Also, I am grateful for the Ellijay church allowing me to use your facilities when I could not focus at home.

Finally, I want to thank each of the following people for believing in us and helping us raise the needed capital to self-publish the first edition of *Undeniable*. I hope that your investment in us will prove to be a blessing to you and many, many more people in the future.

Ardie G.
Betty and Alan G.
Brenda and Ron M.
Brian and Debbie B.
Byron and Carol R.
Carmen F.
Carolyn M.
Carolyn and Max H.
Carolyn B.
Cathy K.
Chule W.
Colleen and Don B.
Dan and Cheryl C.
Daniel F.
Dave and Jackie D.
David T.
David and Sharon E.
Deborah and Joe F.
Dick and Karen L.

Dominic and Georgie S.
Doug and Marie B.
Ed and Sara C.
Ed and Mallory B.
George and Yvonne B.
Greg and Pam B.
Greg and Gina C.
Heidi N.
Heidi G.
Jarod and Beth T.
Jay and Alison C.
Jeff and AnneMarie F.
Jeffrey and Erin S.
Jennifer and Max M.
Jeremy S.
Judy W.
Kalvin and Kristine F.
Keith and Carissa W.
Kenneth D.
Kevin and Vicki W.
Kris and Mary Ann Y.
Larry and Emelia S.
Lester and Lynn M.
Lou and Evelyn M.
Lumina H.
Marimae A.
Marlyn and Loren V.
Paul M.
Paul R.
Ralph and Beatrice N.
Ray A.
Rebecca and Luke S.
Rebecca Z.
Rhoda L.

Robert H.
Sayward C.
Scott A.
Shannon and Keila P.
Steve and Rose P.
Suzy F.
Terrie and Lyle F.
Wendi S.
Many Anonymous Supporters